Priscilla, (White)
Queen of the Desert

gender culture
sexuality

William J. Spurlin
General Editor

Vol. 6

PETER LANG
New York • Washington, D.C./Baltimore • Bern
Frankfurt am Main • Berlin • Brussels • Vienna • Oxford

Damien W. Riggs

Priscilla, (White) Queen of the Desert

Queer Rights/Race Privilege

PETER LANG
New York • Washington, D.C./Baltimore • Bern
Frankfurt am Main • Berlin • Brussels • Vienna • Oxford

Library of Congress Cataloging-in-Publication Data

Riggs, Damien W.
Priscilla (White), queen of the desert: queer rights/race privilege /
Damien W. Riggs.
p. cm. — (Gender, sexuality, and culture, ISSN 1528-6525; v. 6)
Includes bibliographical references.
1. Gay rights—Australia. 2. Racism—Australia. 3. Postcolonialism—
Australia. I. Title.
HQ76.8.A8R54   306.76'608900994—dc22   2006018974
ISBN 0-8204-8658-2 (hardcover)
ISBN 0-8204-8657-4 (paperback)
ISSN 1528-6525

Bibliographic information published by **Die Deutsche Bibliothek**.
Die Deutsche Bibliothek lists this publication in the "Deutsche
Nationalbibliografie"; detailed bibliographic data is available
on the Internet at http://dnb.ddb.de/.

Cover concept by Amy Patterson

The paper in this book meets the guidelines for permanence and durability
of the Committee on Production Guidelines for Book Longevity
of the Council of Library Resources.

© 2006 Peter Lang Publishing, Inc., New York
29 Broadway, New York, NY 10006
www.peterlang.com

All rights reserved.
Reprint or reproduction, even partially, in all forms such as microfilm,
xerography, microfiche, microcard, and offset strictly prohibited.

Printed in the United States of America

Dedicated to the memory of Precilla Choi,
dear friend and colleague.

❦ Contents

General Editor's Foreword by Dr. William Spurlin	ix
Foreword by Dr. Fiona Nicoll	xi
Preface	xv
Acknowledgments	xix
1 Introduction	1
2 Colonial Contexts	17
3 Injured Identities	31
4 Unearned Moral Authority	47
5 What's Love Got to Do with It?	75
6 Possessive Investments	91
Postscript	115
References	119

General Editor's Foreword

In the contemporary world, we have come to understand gender and sexuality as shifting sites of signification. Unlike their traditional constructions tied to the expression of an inner self or essence under a humanist paradigm, postmodern theory, feminism, and academic queer theory have enabled radical rethinking of gender and sexuality as multiple, fluid, variable, contingent, and contextual as they operate under a variety of cultural, historical, rhetorical, and ideological conditions. These fields of inquiry have also helped to denaturalize any causal, normative relation proffered *between* gender and sexuality, exposing these relations as political and deeply imbricated within a heteronormative social order. In particular, academic queer theory, as a mode of analysis and critique, and with its emphasis on the proliferation of social differences, has helped to challenge identic fixity and has enabled more complex theorizations of gender and sexual identity in relation to other sites of subjective identification, including, but not limited to, race, class, geopolitical spatialization, and national affiliation.

This Series is a forum for the critical investigation and analysis of the contested terrain between culture, gender, and sexuality. The books collected in the Series are productive of new directions in queer studies and gender studies as they critically examine the relation(s) between culture and gender and/or sexuality in a range of historical periods, past as well as contemporary. Some projects retheorize gender in relation to, or its constitution through, sexuality, race, class, or culture. Other books are studies of sexuality and sexual identity that produce new understandings of gender, or are broad inquiries into culture that raise compelling implications for the ways in which we think about gender and sexuality as we begin a new century.

While the Series has been influenced by a previous decade productive of queer theorizing, the lines of inquiry undertaken in its aftermath by the authors collected here are both numerous and exciting. For instance, more comparative work and further analyses of gender and sexuality in postcolonial contexts will enable critique of the Euroamerican biases of gender and queer inquiry, while calling attention to their undertheorization in postcolonial studies to the extent that gender and sexuality remain contained within heteronormative frames of reference. The breaking down of national borders, made possible by heightened diasporic migration, the impact of economic globalization, the rapid dissemination of texts and culture worldwide, and the explosion of information technology, further impinge on our traditional understandings of gender and sexuality while continuing to radically transform them. The books in this Series represent highly theoretical engagements with gender and sexuality through a broad range of interdisciplinary inquiry, including anthropology, literary studies, history, psychology, and other areas of the humanities and social sciences. Each volume, as well as the Series as a whole, will make a unique contribution to furthering our understandings of gender and sexuality as categories of analysis and their complex and multiple configurations in the vast, historically specific network(s) of codes, symbols, and signifying practices we have come to understand as culture.

William J. Spurlin
University of Sussex

○₃ Foreword

This book is a lucid and timely intervention within the fields of whiteness studies, critical psychology and queer theory and rights activism. The author's capacity to synthesise existing scholarship across a range of disciplines including history, psychology, law, and cultural studies and apply this to illuminate contemporary cultural texts and activist practices produces an argument that is not only persuasive but also induces unsettling reflections upon the white readers' own conceptual frameworks and everyday practices. The argument woven through this often forensic analysis of queer identity politics is that unexamined and self-interested assumptions about those we wish to recruit to our cause as well as those we define as our 'oppressors' seriously limit the capacity of queer white people to contribute to the 'postcolonising' struggles of Indigenous and other Australians racialised as non-white (see Moreton-Robinson, 2003).

The book begins with a discussion of racialised representation in the iconic and popular Australian cinematic text *The Adventures of Priscilla, Queen of the Desert*. To provide a historical context for the central role and power accorded to whiteness in this and other popular representations of queer subjectivities, Riggs demonstrates how colonial laws relating to male homosexuality promoted a range of 'aspirational practices' that encouraged queer men and women to invest in a racialised construct of the nation as a white possession. This brings the underside of late twentieth century myths of Australia as a multicultural and reconciled nation powerfully into view, demonstrating the inadequacy of any version of queer theory and activism that attempts to establish parallels or suggest commensurabilities between the experiences of queer white men and women and those of Indigenous and other colonised or formerly colonised subjects, whether queer or straight.

Riggs then turns his focus to psychological theories of identity. He explains that psychology's understanding of identity as a *property* of individuals which is vulnerable to injury prevents an appreciation of identity as a set of collectively held and embodied social practices which might well (and often do!) entail unethical competition between individuals claiming injury on different (and incommensurable) grounds such as racism, homophobia and sexism. In a context that has seen Australian Prime Minister John Howard strategically reclaim and reshape the rhetoric of the explicitly racist former One Nation leader, Pauline Hanson, under the guise of a defensive posture within a global war on terror, Riggs' subsequent dissection of the disingenuous rhetoric of 'reverse discrimination' could not be more timely.

Drawing on the work of Wendy Brown and others, the author then addresses problems associated with psychology being posited as the primary ground of appeal against state violence that has historically constructed queers as 'abnormal'. It is argued that such appeals neglect to address the productive power of the state in *normalising* certain versions of queer identities. Under the current neo-liberal regime of power this means that queers are forced to prove injury through homophobic representations or practices. Such injury is treated as though it is perpetrated by *individuals* against claimants who are also constructed as *individuals* rather than by and against members of collectivities that are always already racialised. This prevents consideration of the shared investments in institutionalised discrimination from which all white people benefit regardless of whether we are individually guilty of racist representations or practices.

The implicitly racialised dimensions of queer activism are further pursued through an interesting analysis of battles for moral authority in relation to queer marriage rights. Riggs demonstrates how analogies drawn between opposition to queer marriage and laws prohibiting inter-racial marriage in the Southern States of the US and Apartheid era-South Africa become a point over which white queers jostle for moral authority. Readers are able to recognise ourselves as raced and gendered stakeholders in the issue at stake as Riggs sensitively teases out the different strands of such debates and presents moral outrage itself as a technique for representing a virtuous white self. Such competition over the right to occupy the subject position of the 'good white queer', he points out, paradoxically works against the recognition and support of Indigenous sovereignty struggles over the very ground on which such debates are staged.

As well as excluding alternative forms of relationships between white queers, competitive claims to moral authority marginalise those Indigenous and other subjects racialised as non-white (both queer and straight) who seek to elaborate alternatives to the white middle class nuclear family norm. It is in this context that Riggs critiques queer campaigns that posit property rights and access to reproductive technologies as the central issues at stake for failing to engage with the different histories and experience that Indigenous Australians and other demonised groups such as asylum seekers have with institutions dispensing healthcare, justice and housing. A careful discussion of the queer parenting rights slogan 'Love Makes a Family' underscores this point, highlighting the way discourses of love work to facilitate the access of white queers to privilege as members of a 'national family' which has aggressively excluded asylum seekers in recent years and consistently refused to acknowledge and redress the illegal possession of Indigenous countries. This has brought tragic consequences for those removed from their Aboriginal families through policies and practices of assimilation that were often executed in the name of Christian 'love'. Riggs argues it is necessary for queer white people to come to terms with our possessive investment in the particular form of love embodied in the white middle-class nuclear family and to acknowledge the hatreds this attachment engenders if we are to participate in the project of 'undoing' the global Empire against which the project of post-colonising Australia must now contend.

Finally the reader is asked to consider the racialised reflection in the mirror of queer theory and activism. To what extent is this reflection a product of the materiality of identity conceived not as individual property but rather as a function of the racial privilege accorded to white bodies? In seeking a 'positive' reflection in the mirror do we not as white queers seek the sanction of a state based on a myriad of exclusionary techniques aimed at Indigenous and others racialised as non-white? No answers to these questions are provided to settle the reader's uneasy conscience. Instead the book returns to the point at which it began: with a scene from *Priscilla* in which three white drag queens stand on the edge of a chasm, surrounded by what only appears to be an infinite expanse of empty space and contemplate what it means to belong and to be at home in this place.

I am convinced that in addition to finding a home on academic bookshelves, *Priscilla, (white) queen of the desert* will become an indispensable and well-worn handbook for white queer activists seeking to understand the material investments, ethical complexities and affective ambivalence entailed in engaging with those straight and queer subjects who are currently relegated to the margins of privilege in post-colonising societies such as Australia, New Zealand, Canada and the United States.

Dr. Fiona Nicoll, author, *From Diggers to Drag Queens: Configurations of Twentieth Century Australian Identity,* Pluto Press, 2001.

ଓଃ Preface

The story behind this book is one that I believe worthy of elaboration, as it may help illustrate to the reader why it became evident to me that this book needed to be written. For the past four years I have been engaged in research on race and whiteness in Australia. This came about as a result of what is by now a familiar trope within the field of whiteness studies, namely white people such as myself actually 'getting' that we benefit from white race privilege, and that this is something for which we must be accountable. I will not repeat that 'epiphanic moment' here, but mention it so as to allude to the early thinking that informed this book.

At the same time as conducting research on race and whiteness in Australia, my partner and I began to provide care for a child who is a ward of the state. In doing so as two white gay men, we experienced a myriad of experiences–some good, some bad–as do all parents. This led me to a second research area–that of lesbian and gay parenting. Through writing and publishing in that area, I realised at times that I was so busy compartmentalising my work on whiteness and my work on parenting that I was failing to see precisely how my privilege as a white person was informing my writing as a *white gay male*. One particular instance of this occurred when I was asked to write a chapter for a book on lesbian, gay, bisexual, transgender and queer (LGBTQ) psychology on the topic of whiteness in LGBQ psychology. My initial response was that I was unsure how to do that–how could I bring my two research areas together, and what would it mean to do so?

This question reminded me of a dilemma that had plagued my early research on race and whiteness, and one that I had largely (and conveniently) managed to sidestep–that of the 'multiplicities of whiteness'. In my early research, I had found it difficult to account for my location as white *and* gay *and* male. I kept coming back to a feeling of 'yes but'—yes I have privilege, but I still am discriminated against as a gay man. What I was failing to grapple with and theorise was that I had the wrong 'yes but'—yes I experience discrimination, but I do so as a white person. Trying (and eventually succeeding) to write the chapter for the LGBTQ psychology book challenged me to engage in a theorisation of race in conjunction with gender and sexuality.

At first this took the form of 'intersections', where I explored what it meant to inhabit a number of identities that intersected—this was a bit like a formula—baseline of whiteness equals privilege, minus being gay equals less privilege etc. This initial work was again framed by the discipline of psychology, within which my work is primarily located. It was important for me to engage in this examination of intersections within the context of psychology, primarily because the discipline rarely does so. Yet it was ultimately too simplistic in the sense that it was like shooting fish in a barrel (psychology being a relatively easy target for critiques of individualism), and whilst writing in the first person, it did not really challenge me to interrogate my own privilege, rather than simply state it as rhetoric (e.g., 'I benefit from race privilege too').

I wanted to continue my focus on psychology, because I believe that the discipline holds considerable sway over how white people understand ourselves in colonial nations, and also because I think the discipline has a lot to be accountable for in regards to the production of privilege and oppression. But I wasn't satisfied by simply treating the discipline as a site at which to poke a stick—I wanted to actually look at what it means to be a white queer person. Hence in the present research I have sought to look at the conjuncture of queer and privilege as *one* site (i.e., an always already racialised sexuality), rather than as the 'intersections of identities'. The reader will obviously be the ultimate arbiter of my success in this regard, but I do believe that this text contributes a great deal towards shifting debates over rights and identities, and moving them towards an engagement with accountability that is neither rehearsed nor generalisable.

As such, this text focuses primarily on the context of Australia, but I extend my argument in places in order to explore the ways in which the issues that I raise are played out within the context of the US, and how there are at times considerable overlaps in regards to queer rights/race privilege across colonial settings. As a result, I believe that the broad brushes of the text will strike resonances across a range of colonial settings, as it examines what it means to claim rights in the face of colonial histories–histories that are at times denied or ignored.

As a result of my own location as a white person living in a colonial nation, my aim within this book is to engage in a form of accountability that is founded upon a recognition of the sovereignty of the Indigenous people upon whose land I live. My politics and activism within this book thus represents an express engagement with the fact of Indigenous sovereignty, and as such my discussion of queer rights/race privilege is always already a product of this engagement, something that I believe has been largely lacking within queer theorising and politics, both in Australia and abroad (Barnard, 2003, and Nicoll, 2001, being notable exceptions). As a result, this text is neither presented as a solution to the issue of queer white privilege, nor as simply an attack on queer rights more broadly. Rather, it is a call for further thought and engagement with the need for accountability, and in particular, for those of us who identify as white queer people to begin the work of examining what it means to occupy a privileged position.

ॐ Acknowledgments

I begin by acknowledging the sovereignty of the Kaurna people, the First Nations people upon whose land I live in Adelaide, South Australia. Not only is it protocol to acknowledge the traditional owners of the land upon which I live, but such an acknowledgment of sovereignty is also foundational to my work as a white academic living in a colonial nation.

This book is the result of the coming together of a number of interrelated projects, and as such I owe a great debt to a number of people who shaped my thinking in the process. Primary among these are Fiona Nicoll, Aileen Moreton-Robinson, Derek Hook, Martha Augoustinos, Victoria Clarke, Gordon Walker, Liz Peel, Catherine Butler and Liz Short. Special thanks must also go to Amy Patterson, not only for her intellectual engagement, but also for conceiving such wonderful artwork for the cover.

I could not have produced this piece of work without the intellectual insights afforded by the work of those above, and also Judith Butler, Sara Ahmed, Ian Barnard and Wendy Brown–their work continues to challenge me to think critically not only about my location as a white queer person living in a colonial nation, but also about my politics as a white academic attempting to theorise race/gender/sexuality.

I have also been fortunate to benefit from two intellectual spaces in Australia within which critical thought on race and whiteness are fostered. The first of these is the Australian Critical Race and Whiteness Studies Association (www.acrawsa.org.au), which continues to demonstrate its key importance in the context of a colonial nation such as Australia. The second is the Whiteness Research Group at the University of Adelaide, of which I am a member. To Alia, Kathleen, Jane, Marg, Sonja, Ann and Andrew–I am immensely grateful for your ongoing intellectual rigour and engagement.

Thanks of course must go to William Spurlin for seeing the merit in this project and for agreeing to include it in his book series for Peter Lang. Phyllis Korper, Bernadette Shade and Sophie Appel at Peter Lang all made this a truly enjoyable publishing experience and I thank them for their assistance and patience.

I would also like to thank Celia Kitzinger and Sue Wilkinson, whose engagement with my ideas in Chapter Four, despite being ones that they largely disagreed with, have helped to strengthen the chapter and clarify my argument.

Earlier versions of chapters in this book were previously published in peer-reviewed journals including *Journal of Community and Applied Social Psychology, Australian Psychologist, Asylum, Journal of Australasian Studies, International Journal of Critical Psychology* and *Gender Forum*. I thank the editors and reviewers of these journals for critical commentary, and the publishers for allowing their updated inclusion in this book.

My heartfelt thanks go to my friends and family, for allowing me the time and space in which to write this book, for thought-provoking conversations over its contents, and for understanding the pressures that book writing entails.

Finally, none of this could have been done without Greg, and our child Gary, who help me to make sense of why it is that rights are both so important, and yet so fraught.

Extract from an article by Celia Kitzinger and Sue Wilkinson as it appears on pages 60-62, originally published in 2004 in *Feminism and Psychology, 14,* 127-150, is reprinted by permission of Sage Publications Inc. Extract from an article by Robin Wiegman as it appears on pages 35-36, originally published in 1999 in *Boundary 2, 26,* 115-150, is reprinted by permission of Duke University Press.

෴ 1 Introduction

Speaking about racism, heterosexism or sexism is never an easy thing to do. Speaking about all three of them *at the same time*, without either running them together or ignoring their overlaps, can at times seem like an impossibility, particularly when academic writing must often conform to particular conventions in regards to intelligibility and generalisability. But difficulties such as these are, I believe, more precisely a product of the research questions we ask, and the politics we engage in, rather than the result of anything that makes it inherently impossible to speak *simultaneous*ly about the ways in which oppression and privilege are played out in relation to race, gender and sexuality.

One of the particular causes of the problems identified above in regards to researching intersecting identities is implicit to the opening paragraph itself. There I speak as though there is a 'we' that engages in certain practices. I implicitly refer to a coherent research community that looks at oppression and privilege in certain ways. My claiming of a location within this particular 'we' is a product of my own privilege as a white person living in a colonial nation. To speak from the position of 'we' is to speak from the comfort of the third person plural, believing that my location as a knowing subject is unlikely to be challenged (Nicoll, 2000). Yet increasingly this is not the case. People who have historically been positioned as objects of 'our' research continue to speak back: they continue to refuse to accept the imposition of the third person plural as an acceptable way of speaking.

Research such as that conducted by Indigenous scholars in Australia (e.g., Moreton-Robinson, 2000; 2003; 2004a) and African-American scholars in the US (e.g., hooks, 1981; 1989) continues to challenge white academics such as myself to rethink how we are invested in the identity claims that we make, and how this reflects the privileged location that we occupy—privilege that results from living in what Aileen Moreton-Robinson terms a 'postcolonising' rather than 'postcolonial' nation. Moreton-Robinson proposes "the verb postcolonizing to signify the active, the current and the continuing nature of the colonizing relationship that positions [Indigenous people] as belonging but not belonging" (2003, p. 38). Moreton-Robinson contrasts this with the more common term "postcolonial", which she suggests is not appropriate in the Australian context, as "Indigenous belonging challenges the assumption that Australia is postcolonial because [Indigenous] relation to land [what Moreton-Robinson terms an 'ontological belonging'] is omnipresent, and continues to unsettle non-Indigenous belonging based on illegal dispossession" (p. 24).

Critiques of white/colonising forms of knowledge (such as those presented by Moreton-Robinson) demand an engagement with what it means for white people to research oppression and privilege in postcolonising nations. For myself, this has challenged me to examine what it means to write as a white middle-class gay male, and how this must inform my own research on queer rights claims. Speaking about queer rights, particularly through the lens of queer theory, requires white people who identify as queer to examine how our experiences of oppression in regards to sexuality will always be shaped in a relationship to the privileges that we hold simply by being white people. Yet such a requirement must entail more than simply stating 'yes, I benefit from race privilege too'. What it instead necessitates is an examination of how white queer subjectivities are formed simultaneously through privilege and oppression, and it is to the attendant implications of this for the rights claims of white queer people that I speak within this book.

Writing Queer: Identity Claims and Race Privilege

Throughout this book I use the term 'queer' rather than the perhaps more common moniker 'LGBTI', in order to refer to *practices* rather than *identities*. Thus as William Spurlin (2005) has suggested, 'queer' may be understood as referring to a practice or mode of critique of heteronormative binaries, rather than referring to a particular identity claim (such as 'lesbian' or 'gay'). This focus on queer as a mode of being that centres on critique is one that I believe holds potential for countering normalising understandings of non-heterosexual identities, which often see such identities as reflecting a stable, internal (and indeed often biological) way of being in the world.

One of the problems that I see with talking about identities is that there is a tendency to see identities as a 'bottom line argument'. In other words, the 'existence' of certain 'identity types' (e.g., butch or femme) or 'identity configurations' (e.g., gay or straight) tends to result in the reification not only of these types or configurations, but also of the very category of sexuality itself. Of course, for me to claim a position as a speaking subject within this book is to some degree to speak from *within* the category of sexuality. But this does not necessarily have to lead me to take claims about identity as being foundational–it does not need to be the case that by calling myself queer (or gay, or anything else for that matter), there is a subsequent identity that inheres to that label. The word 'queer', I think, lends itself well to resisting any slippage into notions of a reified identity, and thus may encourage the reader to engage with my focus on the *social practices* that produce particular forms of intelligible subjects.

It is important to clarify here from the onset that I do not believe it to be the case that references to race operate in the same way as references to sexuality. My own politics on race as a white person, drawn as they are from an engagement with the work of scholars in the field of critical race and whiteness studies (e.g., Haggis, 2005; Moreton-Robinson, 2000; Nicoll; 2000), is one that takes racism as a foundational aspect of white subjectivities in colonial nations. This is a point that I will explore further in Chapter Six, but it should suffice to say here that whilst I subscribe to a constructionist position in regards to race, I am concerned with the very real privileges and oppressions that result from race as an organising principle within colonial nations. Thus again my focus on social practices is a useful one–it reminds us not to pay yet more attention to the 'individual racist', but rather to examine how racism structures the lives of all people living in colonial nations– whether that be to privilege or to oppress.

To speak of the term 'queer' (and queer theory more broadly) is thus to recognise that whilst it often refers implicitly to *white* queers/queer theory, as Barnard (2003) so rightly suggests, it may nonetheless represent one potential way in which normative binaries of self/other, white/black, straight/queer may be unsettled, without requiring the dismissal of racism/heterosexism/sexism. This is not of course to suggest that there is anything inherently subversive about identifying as queer or writing queer theory. Rather, my point here is that the critique of heterosexual hegemony provided by queer theory can be usefully brought to bear upon white hegemony under heteropatriarchy (see also Riggs & Walker, 2004). Not only may such an approach contribute to the queering of white privilege itself, but also to an interrogation of *white queer privilege*–something that queer rights campaigns on the whole have most often failed to do.

To return to my opening paragraph, then, I would suggest that to step away from the third person plural is in part to take on an ethical obligation to engage with the unearned privilege held by those of us who identify as white. This does not prevent white queer people from talking about the discrimination that we face or about the rights claims we may wish to make, but instead requires a more complex analysis of what it means to make such claims in the face of our own privilege. In doing so there is also a pressing need to look at what it may mean to identify as a queer person who is not white. This would not be so as to give white queer people (or white straight people for that matter) yet another opportunity to speak for non-white people. Rather, it represents the potential to reflect back to those of us who identify as white precisely how our race privilege operates, and at whose expense it may come.

To speak of queer in the same breath as privilege is thus to engage in an analysis of how white queers are racialised (Barnard, 2003). As such, an analysis of queer rights/race privilege becomes not a form of identity politics whereby we would look at rights claims as problems of addition: white racial identity + queer identity + middle-class identity etc. Rather, to look at queer and privilege simultaneously is to engage in precisely the work that forms the heart of the queer political endeavour: to challenge how binaries operate through exclusion, how normative identity claims come as a result of oppression, and how particular historical assumptions continue to inform the ways in which discourses of difference circulate within colonial nations.

In addition to my focus on what it means to engage in queer politics as a white person in Australia, I am also interested in looking at how queer politics are gendered in particular ways. Here my interest is in examining how particular forms of queer representation achieve hegemony, and how these may, or may not, resist normative forms of gendered embodiment as they are currently configured under white heteropatriarchy (Riggs, 2005a). In writing about gender as a white gay man I am thus interested in exploring how the first and last descriptors in this subject position may often result in a range of unearned privileges that greatly outweigh the oppression that occurs as a result of the central descriptor. Whilst queer politics have necessarily focused on discrimination that results from the marginalisation of queer sexualities, my question is as to whether this focus may represent a failure to examine how such sexualities may still often be highly reliant upon particular normative assumptions around gender and race.

Similarly, whilst my focus in this book is on the privileges that white queer people may hold, I am mindful that the category 'queer people' refers to a very broad range of people whose experiences are not commensurable. To write this book as a white gay man means something very different to what it would mean to write a similar book as a white transgendered person or a white bisexual person (for example). My intention within this book is thus not to collapse categories of queer so as to suggest that all white queer people benefit from race privilege in the same ways, but rather to explore some of the *potential* ways in which queer privilege may operate. In doing so I acknowledge that my own writing is itself an act of privilege and I am thus mindful of the forms of hegemony that may well be perpetuated through this book, written as it is by but one white queer person who in places speaks of the category 'white queer' as if it were a simplistic descriptive category that is not itself problematic. My intention in saying this is not to nod towards incommensurability and then explain it away, but instead to acknowledge that it always already shapes this text, and that it is not something from which I can (or should) attempt to escape—it is something that I must continue to interrogate.

Queer Rights in a 'Postcolonising' Context

Whilst, as I have already mentioned, the primary focus of this book is to bring the aforementioned multiple points of enquiry (i.e., race, gender and sexuality) to bear primarily upon the example of queer rights claims in Australia, I extend this at certain junctures to demonstrate the overlaps between rights claims in the US and Australia. In doing so I am mindful of the many differences between the two countries in regards to racial and queer politics, but at the same time I am most interested in the almost uniform neglect within queer politics in both nations in regards to a sustained engagement with issues of sovereignty and colonisation.

This gap in regards to colonisation in both theory (Nicoll, 2001, being an important exception) and practice is thus my starting place in Chapter Two. In that chapter I outline the context of colonisation in Australia, and I sketch out how this has produced particular queer white identities in a historical context. In that chapter I also outline the terms of references that I use throughout this book, and I pay particular attention to what it means to be located as a white queer person living in Australia who exists in a relation to particular legal practices in regards to racialised, gendered and sexualised hierarchies. This leads me to suggest that queer identities are produced as particular social practices that require interrogation for the privileges that they may assume.

In the chapters subsequent to Chapter Two I thus explore some of the identity claims that are made by white queers, and how these inform current queer rights activism. I do this as I believe that understanding how identity claims operate may help those of us who identify as white queers to develop political strategies that need not be so reliant upon the forms of identity politics that currently shape rights claims. The problems that underpin identity claims in regards to sexuality, as I outlined earlier, suggest to me that there is a pressing need to consider alternate ways of understanding our selves, and in particular to do so by understanding how the very concept of self (of which identity is an extension) signifies a social, rather than individual practice.

I begin the work of elaborating how individualistic identity claims may work to the disservice of queer rights in Chapter Three, by focusing on Wendy Brown's (1994) work on rights claims, and in particular on her suggestion that rights claims which take as their starting place the 'injured identity' of the plaintiff may fail to examine how this positions plaintiffs in particular ways. By looking at social scientific representations of queer rights claims, alongside those made by queer rights advocates themselves, I provide an account of how the claiming of rights by queer white people does not pay significant attention to issues of race and racism. By locating the 'injured identity' claims of white queer people alongside similar claims made by white people more broadly in both Australia and the US, I demonstrate the problems associated with assuming this type of identity when making claims for state sanction.

This focus on issues of identity leads into Chapter Four, where I turn my attention to what Alan Běrubě (2001) has termed 'unearned moral authority'. Here I examine the problems that arise when queer rights advocates use particular identity claims that are reliant upon moral judgments in order to warrant their claims to truth. I propose that such moral claims are both highly racialised and highly context specific, and yet are most often not subjected to interrogation by white queers in regards to the moral authority that we claim when speaking from such a position.

In Chapter Five I apply the work of Sara Ahmed (2003) to examine what it means to claim a particular moral identity as a 'good queer' within the context of a postcolonising nation. In particular, I focus on queer parenting rights campaigns that employ the slogan 'Love makes a family', and I elaborate a philosophical framework through which to understand how such slogans demonstrate a substantive logic that configures love as an implicit basis for the identity of certain (white) queers, whilst excluding other people from claiming to 'act from love'. My suggestion in Chapter Five is that white queer parents must be mindful of how we are invested in particular forms of belonging that come as a result of our location within a particular white national imaginary.

In the concluding chapter of the book, I explore the utility of queer theory for understanding queer race privilege, and I engage with the need to develop forms of rights claims that need not be so reliant on the current forms of state sanction available to queer people. In so doing I explore one particular way of understanding how identities may be understood as social practices, and how queer people are always already racialised. In order to do this I elaborate upon a theoretical framework provided by Aileen Moreton-Robinson (2004a), namely what she terms 'the possessive logic of patriarchal white sovereignty'. Her cogent analysis of land rights decisions in Australia demonstrates how white people in Australia are invested in claiming particular forms of belonging and ownership, and how this serves to disavow Indigenous sovereignty. My interest in the framework she provides is twofold: first, to look at what it means to claim belonging as a white queer person in the context of a postcolonising nation, and second, to examine how such claims to belonging may represent a specifically queer investment in the hegemonic practices of the white nation. From there I conclude with some thoughts on alternate approaches to queer rights campaigns within the context of a postcolonising nation.

In order to introduce the reader to the key motifs of the book, I spend the remainder of this chapter exploring one particular example of how white queer representation is configured through particular racialised politics. Taking the title of the book as its starting place, the following section explores how race privilege operates within the movie *The Adventures of Priscilla, Queen of the Desert,* and I elaborate how this may help us to understand the limitations of white queer identity politics as they are currently configured under white heteropatriarchy.

Priscilla and the Racialisation of Queer Identities

Released in 1994, and written and directed by a white gay Australian man–Stephan Elliot–*The Adventures of Priscilla, Queen of the Desert* is a campy take on the life of three white queers who travel together through the outback to perform a drag show in Alice Springs. Along the way the three main characters meet a number of different people from a range of backgrounds, some of whom become part of the story as it progresses. Whilst the film is primarily the story of the three main characters, and their own queer identities and forms of representation, I believe it can afford us particular insight into how white queer politics and identity claims operate in Australia. To supplement my reading of the film, I also engage with one particular academic paper (Padva, 2000) that has taken up the 'cause' of the film, which is depicted in the paper as an example of the 'politicization of camp subculture'. Through a reading of these two texts, I will highlight how white queer politics in Australia may at times trade on particular hegemonic forms of representation, and how they may as a result fail to interrogate white privilege.

There are two particular areas of symbolism that I wish to focus on in regards to *Priscilla*, and there is a third area–that of white queer belonging–that I will return to in the concluding chapter of this book. My first point of interest is to explore how white queers are at times seemingly placed outside of oppression. The second is to look at how white queerness may be seen within the movie to co-opt Indigeneity, and how this is simultaneously challenged by Indigenous people. These two foci will be interspersed with my own responses to the aforementioned paper that focuses on the politics of the film (Padva, 2000), in order to more closely examine how *Priscilla* has been read, and how such readings may similarly neglect to engage in an interrogation of the film's raced and gendered assumptions.

In regards to my first point of inquiry, I focus on one particular symbol of Australiana that is used within the film, namely, the kangaroo. More specifically, I am interested in two instances where the image of a dead kangaroo would seem to suggest a particular representation of queerness within the film. In the first instance, the three main characters find themselves lost in the middle of the desert when their bus ('Priscilla') breaks down. One character, Bernadette, goes out in search of assistance. As her search goes on, Bernadette finds herself in increasingly isolated areas of the desert. Luckily, she is fortunate to see a vehicle heading towards her. She manages to flag it down, and is given a ride by the elderly white couple who drive it. Unfortunately for Bernadette, she must sit in the back of the vehicle along with a dead, and rather fly-blown, kangaroo. Things get worse upon her return to the bus when she fetches her two travel companions to meet her saviors, only for them to drive off in a cloud of dust when one of the queer men appears in drag, whilst the other is covered in pink paint. The elderly couple by implication are depicted as homophobic or otherwise uncaring about the plight of the three stranded characters and their bus.

The second time we see the symbol of the kangaroo is later that night, when an Indigenous man comes across the three characters. He invites them back to his campsite, where a large group of Indigenous people are sitting near an open fire over which a kangaroo roasts. When the three characters arrive at the campsite they are depicted as feeling somewhat uneasy about the stares of the Indigenous people, and unsure about how to engage in social interaction. This appears to be broken down when, following on from one Indigenous man playing a guitar, the three characters perform a number in drag for their (seemingly appreciative) Indigenous audience.

There appears to me to be a stark contrast made in the film between the symbol of the dead kangaroo as it is associated with the elderly white couple, and the roasting of the kangaroo by the Indigenous people. In the first instance, the kangaroo represents discrimination against the character of Bernadette, identified in the film as transgendered. She is forced to sit next to the dead carcass, and for her trouble is abandoned by her would be white saviors. Here we see a contrast between the white queer characters, who are the ones being abandoned, and the white (nominally heterosexual) characters, who are doing the abandoning. The next time we see the symbol of the kangaroo, however, we see the three white queer characters in the process of 'being saved'. Here the kangaroo may be taken to represent substance or aid offered, as opposed to the discrimination that occurs when first we see the symbol. The white queer characters are not only depicted as being saved by the Indigenous character, but appear to be relatively straightforwardly welcomed (or indeed even embraced) by the group of Indigenous people. Here the symbol of the kangaroo (to be shared as food) implicitly aligns the white queers 'on the side' of the Indigenous people–as engaged in a form of mutual recognition or understanding that stands in opposition to the imagery of the dead and rotting kangaroo associated with the elderly white couple. White queers in this sense are depicted as being on the side of 'the good'–of those who are oppressed, rather than those who are doing the oppressing.

Likewise, within the paper written by Gilad Padva (2000), there is an implicit assumption that white queers are somehow beyond oppression, or more precisely, that they do not engage in acts of oppression towards other groups of people. In his preliminary discussion of how camp representations can destabilise normative forms of representation, Padva suggests that the:

> proto-camp gestures developed by men like the mollies [an 18th century term used by same-sex attracted men to refer to themselves] may have actually worked to displace the epistemological clarity of dominant codes of identity. Therefore,

the early modern origins of English camp may actually have been those well-informed political practices that deployed the representation of the body against the growing bourgeois attempt to shape and control the subject. (p. 223)

Whilst interesting, Padva's argument makes the implicit suggestion that early English camp was inherently distinct from a bourgeois identity, and thus did not attempt to 'shape and control the subject'. The question that I would ask of this is, exactly which men were 'well-informed' in their engagement with 'proto-camp gestures', and how may these men themselves have been, if not bourgeois subjects, at least subjects who stood to benefit from being (presumably) white men living in a society that accorded significant privilege to white men. Padva's imagery of 'proto-camp' men may thus be seen to do very little to challenge how such men may have not only been engaged in 'displacing the epistemological clarity of dominant codes of identity', but also in asserting new, and equally oppressive (white, masculine) codes of identity. In other words, to depict white queers as 'displacing' oppressive social practices may demonstrate a failure to examine how white queers similarly stand to benefit from such practices. The quote from Padva thus shares similarities with the example above of the white queers' interaction with the group of Indigenous people, in that both the mollies that Padva refers to, and the white queers in *Priscilla,* are somehow positioned as being removed from oppression in the sense of enacting it against others.

To return to the film again, and to my second point of inquiry in regards to co-option, we may see how particular white queer forms of representation engender a particular logic of reciprocity that is appropriative rather than acknowledging. In the remainder of the storyline relating to the drag performance reported above, the three white queer characters notice during their performance that the Indigenous man who originally found them is merrily dancing along to the performance. This gives them an idea—to make him part of the performance! Thus we see a final set of routines wherein the Indigenous man is clothed in drag, and dances along with the three white queer characters. My concern with this particular representation is that whilst the Indigenous man in the first instance seems to offer a form of aid to the three white queer characters that acknowledges their need for help, their response to this aid is not an acknowledgment in return of the specificity of Indigenous experience, but rather is to some degree appropriative: it reads Indigenous experience *through* white queer experience (and thus in effect co-opts Indigenous experience into white queer experience). Of course my suggestion is not that the Indigenous man did not want to join in the white queers' performance, nor that he or the Indigenous characters were dupes of the performance. Rather, my point is that the form of reciprocity or relationship that is engendered between the two groups (white queers and Indigenous people) is one that appears to be largely directed by the white queers (and their needs), and which does not problematise the white queers as being stranded *upon Indigenous land*. Rather, the white queers reciprocate the aid given to them by the Indigenous man by offering him a role in *their* performance, instead of themselves seeking to reciprocate on terms set by the Indigenous man. As we are given no indication of the Indigenous man's sexual identity, we cannot interpret the accuracy of the white queers' reading of his dancing to the performance, nor what the Indigenous man's engagement with the performance meant *for the man himself*. Instead we are largely left with the viewpoint of the white queers.

Having said all that, there is I believe a great deal of space left open to the white viewer to think about and challenge the particular reading that I believe the film provides. First in this regard, when the white queers join the Indigenous people by the campfire they are depicted as feeling uneasy, a feeling that we see reflected in the alternately inquisitive or disinterested gaze of the Indigenous people. In other words, the white queers *are being seen*, but not on their terms. Second, the Indigenous people who watch the performance largely engage on their terms—we are left unsure as to what their laughter at the performance signifies, and we are shown that their reception of the performance suggests a particular Indigenous reading of white queer. This appears in the incorporation of the performance into the music already being performed by the Indigenous people, where the white performance becomes in part an aspect of the broader Indigenous context of the evening. Finally, and perhaps most importantly, the following day, when he again assists the white queers in returning to their bus and securing a tow truck, the Indigenous man asks of them 'so you actually make money by dressing up like a woman?' This, I would suggest, implicitly reasserts an Indigenous reading of white queer representation, one that challenges the straightforward assumption that Indigenous people can be simplistically incorporated into white readings of Indigeneity. In this sense, white queerness becomes the other to Indigenous identity, rather than reverse.

The challenge that Indigenous sovereignty presents here to the logic of white queerness is, I believe, indicative of the incommensurability that must be taken as a foundation to any dialogue between Indigenous and white people (Haggis, 2005). In other words, rather than simply presuming that a shared ground does exist, it is important that white people acknowledge the differences that shape our experiences (through privilege) as distinct from those of Indigenous people. A failure to engage with such incommensurabilities is evident in Padva's (2000) paper on *Priscilla* and camp representation. Drawing on the work of African American scholar bel hooks (1992), Padva suggests not only that "the (straight) bourgeois attempt to manipulate the (queer) subject is similar to interracial relationships, especially between white dominant culture and black subculture" (p. 222), but also that "[hooks'] claim for revision of black history and ethnic oppression can be associated with a demand for revision of queer history and heterosexist oppression" (p. 223). Here Padva may be seen to engage in a form of co-option, whereby he presumes that the critique of racial oppression (as presented by hooks) can be mapped across to a (nominally white queer) critique of 'heterosexist oppression'. This form of co-option, besides running the risk of denying how white queers benefit from unearned race privilege and how white queers are never outside racism, also appears to depict people as being either queer or black. The question this begs is of course: 'what does this mean for black queers?' Padva's paper thus attempts to make neat work of what in practice is nowhere near as neat: white queer politics are never entirely outside of oppression, and the threat of co-option *by* white queers is the implicit flipside to critiques of the co-option *of* white queers.

Chapter Summary

The brief analysis presented here of both *The Adventures of Priscilla, Queen of the Desert* and the work of Padva (2000) highlights some of the problems facing white queer politics in Australia. My intention has not been to provide a definitive reading of either text, but rather to draw attention to some of the problems that they present for representations of white queers in Australia. Not only does my analysis demonstrate the troublesome ways in which white queers at times engage with race in Australia, but it also highlights some of the assumptions around racialised and gendered privilege that inform queer politics. As three white queer characters, and myself as a white gay man, we experience considerable privilege as a result of our social location. This is something that I believe requires accountability, and something that is not easily theorised away or discounted through recourse to 'good intentions'. Being white and queer in Australia does not place us outside of racism, nor does it mean that our self-representations are not seen as oppressive by those who identify as non-white.

These are of course difficult statements to make, not primarily because they suggest a need to engage in forms of accountability, but rather because they may be read by some as disavowing the need for some form of queer rights, or as overwriting white queer experiences of oppression. These I believe are necessary risks, and ones that I can take precisely because of my white identity. They therefore do not inherently represent examples of me actually 'giving up power', but are rather moments where I enact the very power that comes from being white in a society that privileges white people. So what does this means for a situated queer politics?

First, I think it suggests that there must be much more to white queer politics than simply deconstructing heteropatriarchy. Heteropatriarchy is gendered and racialised as much as it is sexualised, and there is a pressing need to look at how white queers may well be complicit with oppression, even if we attempt to challenge its operations. Second, there is the need to more adequately theorise the relationship that white queers in Australia have to Indigenous sovereignty—how does it form the ground upon which we develop our politics, and what does this mean for the types of politics that we engage in? Third, we must recognise the incommensurable differences that shape white and Indigenous experience, and to pull back from trading on comparisons between racial and sexual/gender oppression. These types of comparisons, I believe, can only serve to marginalise the concerns of non-white people, and render invisible the experiences of queer non-white people. And finally, there is the need to recognise what these incommensurabilities signify: they arise as an outcome of colonisation, and as such they are a challenge to the claims to belonging of white queers. It will not suffice to simply recognise these differences: from this must follow a commitment to examine not what these difference mean *for other people*, but rather how these differences signify the tenuous location of white people in Australia, including white queers.

These are all issues that I will return to through the remainder of this book, and ones that form the heart of its terms of inquiry. To look at queer and privilege simultaneously may at times be uncomfortable work for white queers such as myself, but it is work that is required in order to develop an ethical basis from which to engage in queer rights in the context of a postcolonising nation.

☙ 2 Colonial Contexts

In this chapter I provide a broad outline of the context of colonisation in Australia, and I use this to examine how white queer people have been historically positioned in Australia as both objects and subjects of the law. In so doing I am interested to look at how certain sexual practices have been accorded a relationship to certain identities, and how this may be seen as a precursor to contemporary identity claims in regards to queer politics. More specifically, by outlining how certain sexual practices have been historically positioned within Australian law as initially signifying pathological *behaviours*, and subsequently pathological *identities*, I intend to demonstrate how these historical contingencies serve as uneasy foundations for rights claims made *through the law* by white queers in the present.

In this chapter I also elaborate some of the terms that I use throughout the remainder of the book, and spend some time delineating the scope of my inquiry, and the limitations that it produces. In so doing, I locate white queer rights campaigns in the present within a context of shifting social representations of queer people more broadly, which thus enables me to situate my own analysis of identity claims that takes place in subsequent chapters within a framework that is grounded in the realities of a postcolonising nation such as Australia.

Colonisation, Migration and the Fiction of Terra Nullius

Australia as a nation, and more specifically, Australia as a part of the colonising project of the British Empire, was established upon a series of *a priori* assumptions about landownership and the entitlement of white colonisers to appropriate land from Indigenous people. In contrast to colonial nations such as the United States and New Zealand, where some form of treaty was negotiated with Indigenous people, Australia was 'taken possession of' in the name of King George III, despite an awareness on the part of both Captain Cook and the British monarchy that Australia was already inhabited. The presence of Indigenous owners was circumvented by the declaring of the land as 'Terra Nullius'—as the 'land of no one'. This legal assumption presumed not that the land was literally empty, but that it was legally empty of property owning subjects who held a rightful or recognised claim to ownership. Such an assumption, which required the brutal enforcement of the presumed to be sovereign rights of the British monarchy, has thus informed relationships between Indigenous and white people since first contact.

What the assumption of Terra Nullius signifies in regards to Indigenous people is that the sovereignties of the more than two hundred Indigenous nations that existed in Australia before colonisation were denied. Yet the denial of sovereignty by white colonisers does not mean that the sovereignty of Indigenous people does not continue to exist, nor that Indigenous people have not consistently resisted the theft of their lands (Moreton-Robinson, 2003). Whilst white people may have gained control of much of the land that constitutes Australia through brute force of numbers, and whilst this land is claimed as a possession of the Australian nation state (proclaimed as such in 1901), the existence of Indigenous title to land has not been effectively distinguished. This was shown in the landmark Mabo2 land rights case, where the High Court recognised the inherent rights of Indigenous people to hold title to land as First Nations people. However, this has not been without consequence. Primary of these has been the Howard government's Native Title Amendment Act, 1998, which significantly tightened the requirements for the claiming of land rights as they were originally outlined in the Native Title Act (1993) passed by the previous Labor government. This amendment to the Act was passed in many ways as a response to the findings of the Wik land rights claim, which recognised that Native Title is not inherently extinguished by the granting of a pastoral lease. Findings such as these were seen as constituting a threat to the sovereignty claims of the white nation (and its white pastoralists in particular), hence the passing of the Native Title Amendment Act as a way of curtailing the impact of the Wik finding.

Though since the passing of the Act some land claims have been successful (such as the Miriuwung Gajjerong case), many have not been recognised by the High Court (such as those by the Yarmirr, Fejo and Yorta Yorta First Nations people). In the case of the Yorta Yorta people, the testimony of white pastoralists and anthropologists were used to 'prove' that the Yorta Yorta people had not had 'continuous contact with their lands' and, in Justice Olney's words, that the 'tide of history' had 'washed away' native title (Moreton-Robinson, 2004a). This represents one particular example of the legal fiction of Terra Nullius being used to perpetuate the claiming of ownership by white people, where native title is defined according to the rules of white law, and where the testimony of white people is taken as *a priori* evidence of possession (Moreton-Robinson, 2004a).

It is not only the case, however, that the white Australian nation is claimed through the disavowal of Indigenous sovereignty. Whilst my primary focus within this book is on how white queer rights claims are made within the context of a colonial nation that is founded upon dispossession and genocide, it is also important to recognise that white people in Australia (queer or otherwise) benefit not only from the disavowal of Indigenous sovereignty, but also from particular constructions of national belonging in Australia. Belonging has historically been taken in Australia by white people as referring to the belonging conferred through a relationship to particular norms around identities, whiteness and migrancy.

It is important to elaborate here how I use the terms 'white' and 'whiteness'. To refer to someone as 'white', particularly in the context of Australia, is to refer to them as occupying a particular location in relation to racialised networks of power. To refer to someone as white is not to naively accept that race as a category is useful, or a biological fact, or internally coherent. Rather, to 'recognise race' (as in referring to someone as 'white') is to acknowledge that assumptions of racialised difference continue to inform how we relate to one another as people, and that this is the legacy of a long history of violence that has been perpetuated in the name of imperialism and colonisation against people classified as racial others. To speak of someone as 'being white' is thus to unsettle the norm of white privilege—to refuse to continue to allow those of us who identify or are identified as white a position of normality—to challenge our assumptions of invisibility or 'racelessness', and to locate white people as benefactors within the discriminatory classificatory system that is 'race' (Moreton-Robinson, 2004a; Richards, 1997).

Of course at the same time it is never quite as simple as all that. Many white people will contest their location in regards to a white racial norm. The category white is one that is always changing, and we only need to look back a few decades to see how differing groups of people in Australia were often not considered to be white (Nicolacopoulos & Vassilacopoulos, 2004). My use of the term white is therefore not intended to subsume all non-indigenous people within a catch-all category. Nor is it to attempt to speak for non-indigenous people who do not identify as white. Rather my interest is to acknowledge how oppression and privilege operate in Australia in regards to queer rights advocacy, and in particular to examine how white privilege constitutes the unacknowledged core of white queer rights claims.

To refer to the study of whiteness is thus not to refer to the study of an internal essence, or a biological entity, or to posit a static social fact that is beyond challenge. Rather, to study whiteness is to study the interlocking, complex ways in which white people benefit from white privilege, enshrined as it is in institutional networks that prioritise the values, behaviours and beliefs of dominant group members (Moreton-Robinson, 2000). Whiteness may thus be understood as a form of cultural capital that, whilst being differentially distributed amongst those variously identified as white, does nonetheless come at the expense of the oppression of those who are identified as not being white (Fine, 1997; Hage, 1998).

These above points highlight the specific focus of this book: whilst I *do* pay attention in my analyses to the ways in which a range of non-white people are positioned within the Australian nation, and whilst I explore the implications of this for queer people who do not identify as white, my focus is not on 'breaking whiteness down' so as to look at the minutiae of white identities. Rather, my interest is in regards to the ways that particular identity claims serve the purposes of certain groups of people, with a focus on what this means for the identity claims of white queer people. In the following section I further map out the areas of interest that constitute the primary foci of this book, and I outline some of the terminology that I use throughout the book.

Locating Race, Gender and Sexuality in Colonial Contexts

In this section I further outline the terms that I use throughout this book, and the implications of these terms for examining racialised, gendered and sexualised hierarchies in Australia. In doing so I allude to some of the similarities that I believe exist across a broad range of histories in Australia. My intention here is not to dismiss the specificities of individual experience, but rather to locate these subjective practices within a broader context of imperialism and colonisation. My work here draws on the broad literature on colonial desire, both in Australia and abroad (e.g., Aldrich, 2003; Lane, 1995; Stoler, 1995; Young, 1995), but adds what I think is a much needed dimension—a recognition of the relationship that white people in Australia always already have to Indigenous sovereignty (Nicoll, 2004a), and an examination of the implications of this for studies of gender and sexuality.

Whilst throughout this book I use the term 'queer' to refer primarily to practices rather than identities, I recognise that this term has a very recent, and contextually contingent meaning, and thus is not particularly appropriate for explaining the experiences of (primarily) same-sex attracted men in 'colonial Australia'. At the same time, however, the term more commonly used ('homosexual') is one that sits uncomfortably with my own politics. I thus use the term homosexual when referring to the period in colonial Australia where the law recognised (or indeed created) the category itself. Prior to this time homosexual acts where considered simply to be that—individual, isolated behaviours, rather than as emblematic of an actual 'type' of person (Aldrich, 2003). It is only much more recently that same-sex attracted individuals have been identified by (and adopted) the terms 'lesbian' and 'gay', amongst others. With this explanation of terminology in mind, I hope that the reader will accept my varied use of these terms.

In addition to the terminology of sexuality used within this book, it is important to draw attention to their gendered nature. As I will elaborate in the following sections, laws governing homosexuality (or more precisely, 'sodomy') were primarily directed at men. Thus discussions of 'homosexuality' in the following sections pertain primarily to white men. However, I continue to refer throughout this book to 'white queers' as I believe that early colonial constructions of homosexuality have bestowed a legacy that is often taken up by both white same-sex attracted men and women (albeit in highly differential ways). In order to draw out some of the boundaries of my argument, then, I draw attention to the fact that I make gender explicit in my analysis, and that I recognise the multiple ways in which white race privilege is shaped through discourses of gender.

In regards to my use of the terms 'imperialism' and 'colonisation', I draw upon the work of Maori scholar Linda Tuhiwai Smith (1999), who suggests that the term imperialism may be understood as referring to the:

> Enlightenment spirit which signalled the transformation of economic, political and cultural life in Europe. In this wider Enlightenment context, imperialism becomes an integral part of the development of the modern state, of science, of ideas and of the 'modern' human person. (p. 22)

Imperialism may thus be understood as a way of thinking about the world that is based upon the values of white people. Smith further suggests that colonisation is one specific mode of imperialism: the imposition of one set of beliefs onto another, regardless of the outcome. Indeed, within a binary framework of self and other (where the former is considered superior to the latter), the colonisation of those considered to be different from the majority or dominant group works to automatically position them as other, and thus as 'naturally' inferior. Colonisation is thus a practice of legitimation that is used to justify the worldview of white people, and one that continues to shape the subjectivities of all people in Australia. Thus whilst I use the term 'colonial Australia' to refer to the first hundred years or so of white invasion, this should not be taken as suggesting that Australia is no longer in the process of colonisation: white ways of knowing continue to be privileged, and Indigenous sovereignty continues to be disavowed.

The above explications of imperialism and colonisation thus draw attention to some of the complex ways in which white men and women, heterosexual or otherwise, stand to benefit from racialised hierarchies. My argument within this book for a particular reading of the investments in the white nation that queer people have made since 1788 is thus important in that it demonstrates how a continued focus on the specificities of white queer experience is not sufficient to challenge race privilege. In other words, whilst it is important to acknowledge and explore the multiple ways in which those of us who identify as white are located in relation to discourses of gender, sexuality and class (to name a few), it is also important to examine how white people are often very similarly positioned as a result of our racialised subject positions. This can be exemplified in the development of the term 'homosexual' in colonial Australia. Whilst the term came to be used to describe a group of people, who were labeled as deviant or pathological, it was not taken to be representative of the white race in general. This is in contrast to constructions of Indigenous people as 'sexually available', 'sexually deviant' and otherwise 'perverted', terms that were applied to *all* Indigenous people by white colonisers (Gays and Lesbians Aboriginal Alliance, 1994). Thus my argument in this chapter is that since 1788 white queer individuals have had access to privileges based on their race, and it is to these privileges (and their corollary oppressions of Indigenous people, amongst others) that we must be accountable.

Colonial Contexts: Policing 'the Homosexual'

In this section I provide a brief account of some of the laws that existed in regards to sodomy in colonial Australia, and I elaborate how these laws relate to the broader social morals and values that circulated at the time, particularly as they were configured through the ideologies of imperialism. This account focuses in particular on the three aspects that I elaborate in the following section in regards to white claims to belonging and ownership, namely (a) the normative gendered assumptions that informed colonial law, (b) the varying constructions of sexuality that circulated within colonial Australia, and (c) the racialised power dynamics that encouraged white colonisers to deny the fact of Indigenous sovereignty. These three aspects thus make visible some of the institutionalised practices that render white people complicit with the dispossession and genocide of Indigenous people, regardless of our 'well intentioned' claims (Riggs, 2004a).

As feminist scholars have continued to elaborate, the law is *a priori* designed to protect the status quo under heteropatriarchy (MacKinnon, 2005; Weisberg, 1993). This fact is even more explicitly evident in early colonial law in Australia, which was premised on the assumption that only white men had the necessary faculties (i.e., rationality) required to access and arbitrate legal practice (an assumption that has again been asserted recently in the Yorta Yorta land rights claim; see Moreton-Robinson, 2004a). The law thus held only limited control over the lives of white men, as opposed to the laws that governed the rights of white women, and the laws that controlled the movement, rights and indeed lives of all Indigenous people. Whilst it is true that white men's access to the law was mediated by their status in regards to class and sexual preference, this does not negate the fact that all white men stood to benefit from the normative assumptions of patriarchal law. An example of this comes from a case of sodomy in 1855 presented by Libby Connors (1994, pp. 98-99). In the case the complainant testified that the defendant had "attempt[ed] to commit an unnatural crime". Connors suggests however that "it seems likely that [the complainant and defendant] had had a homosexual relationship", and that the fight between them was a matter of jealousy. The intervention of the law thus only came on the invitation of the complainant: both men (as white men) were otherwise relatively free from the incursions of the law upon their lives. In other words, unless they were 'caught' engaging in sodomy, or brought accusations against one another, white men were presumed to be heterosexual, and thus entitled to full sanction by the law.

The institution of heterosexuality as a foundational assumption of colonial law also granted white women access to the law by *de facto* of their relationship to white men. Obviously this access was greatly mediated by discourses of white women's 'fragility' and 'delicate sensibilities', but, nevertheless, colonial law included statutes to protect the 'virtuousness' of white women. My point here is not to deny the misogyny of the law (colonial or otherwise), or how the law often continues to render lesbians invisible, but rather to point towards the benefits that all white people gain(ed) under the auspice of the law.

Research into relations between white men in colonial Australia has emphasised the central role of discourses of 'mateship' (Aldrich, 2003; Nicoll, 2001). Whilst there continues to be debate over whether mateship as a form of homosociality engendered homosexual relations, or whether the reverse is true (i.e., that homosexual preferences led to mateship), white men stood to benefit in colonial Australia from the racialised sexualisation of non-white men as being inherently predatory and dangerous. Though an extended discussion of the 'politics of passing' will be explored in Chapter Five, it should suffice to say here that unlike white women and Indigenous men and women, white men who engaged in homosexual practices had the 'choice' to engage with discourses of mateship, and thus the potential to mask their sexual preferences. Mateship thus represented for homosexual men the possibility of meeting other homosexual men, and also granted them the privilege that 'mateship networks' engendered. This is evident to some degree in the relative reluctance of colonial courts to convict men charged on accounts of sodomy, or if convicted, to impose the death penalty as the outcome. Thus as Robert Aldrich (2003, p. 238) suggests, the statistics on white men convicted on accounts of sodomy, or indeed executed, "do not give evidence of a particularly vicious campaign against homosexuals". This relative leniency may be contrasted with the sustained campaign of violence that was mounted against Indigenous people, and which continues to be evidenced in the laws and public policy that deny Indigenous sovereignty. Thus whilst colonial Australia was configured through a normative heterosexuality, it still provided privileges and protection for white men who engaged in homosexual acts.

These shifting dynamics of power under early colonial law were thus another way in which white hegemony was maintained through the bodies of individual white men. Though it is true that homosexuality was not legalised in Australia until the late twentieth century, previous amendments to sodomy laws translated into a range of implications for men who engaged in homosexual practices. Some examples of these include amendments to the law in the form of (a) 1828: men convicted of sodomy ceased to lose their property rights, (b) 1883: the death penalty was removed as a punishment for sodomy, and (c) 1860: the increasing introduction of the category 'homosexual' as a means to understanding homosexual practices within the law. In regards to the last point, Aldrich (2003, p. 221) suggests that "by the last decades of the century, colonial society, or at least the judiciary, had constructed homosexual identity as a sexual orientation (rather than simply viewing sodomy as an aberrant act)". This came at a similar time to when white women were granted the ability to own property (in Victoria this occurred in 1883).

These shifts in laws, whilst often accompanied by relatively greater or lesser levels of prosecutions for sodomy (or for lesser offenses such as 'indecent exposure with a male'; see Fogarty, 1992), translated into a shift from a "power based on discipline to one transfigured into normalization" (Stoler, 1995, p. 89). Thus the construction of the category 'homosexual' and its recognition within law courts, alongside the growing rights of white women, meant that white men and women, *regardless of sexuality*, were provided with examples of how to 'approximate the norm'. In other words, the (albeit gradual) extension or securing of rights for all white women and for homosexual white men translated into a context whereby these groups were able to access the privileges automatically accorded to white heterosexual men. In the following section I propose that this increased access to privilege translated into a range of 'aspirational practices' that allowed homosexual white men in particular an increased freedom in determining their status within colonial Australia, and one that was dependent upon the acceptance of normative ideals around race. Whilst this of course did little to challenge the centrality of heterosexuality, it set the scene for white homosexual men in particular to gain 'equality with' their heterosexual counterparts.

Shoring up the White Nation

The previous section in regards to colonial law provides a framework within which to understand how a range of 'aspirational practices' were used to encourage white homosexual men and white women to invest in the white nation. Whilst these practices were most likely not the explicit intention of the law, I believe that they were founded on a particular logic in which individuals are positioned as either objects or subjects of the legal gaze. Amendments to sodomy laws thus produced 'the sodomite' (and later 'the homosexual') as agentic subjects—as recognisable human beings whose claims to rights were in some way acknowledged—which was directly contrasted with the construction of white and Indigenous women (and at times, Indigenous men) as being objects of white men's 'uncontrollable lust' (Fogarty, 1992). By elaborating this point, I hope to demonstrate how white homosexual men were invested in the white nation, and how this worked to recentre normative, masculinised white heterosexuality as the foundation of the nation.

The amendment of sodomy laws in 1828 to allow men convicted of sodomy to retain their property and property rights positioned such men as entitled to property. This, I would suggest, was founded on a logic of ownership, whereby white men (albeit mediated by class and convict status) where *a priori* entitled to own land. Thus whilst men who were convicted may have had less symbolic capital, it still benefited both them and the white nation to include them as citizens (particularly those of wealth). Two examples from colonial law demonstrate how property rights encouraged homosexual men to desire ownership in the context of the white nation. The first example comes again from Connors' (1994) work, where she suggests that courts were less willing to pursue claims of sodomy against men. She proposes that in the early colonial period this was due to the fact that as many white men as possible were needed in the workforce (to secure white possession of land, and to defend white land claims against Indigenous people). The law was thus reluctantly used to deny homosexual men's ability to own land (even if the men themselves were not eligible to actually own land, and regardless of the prohibition on sodomy and homosexuality, it was important for the nation to secure sovereign rights to land, particularly as the fiction of Terra Nullius was actively contested by the fact of Indigenous sovereignty as evidenced by the ongoing resistances of Indigenous people).

This leads me to the second, more specific example. In the case mentioned earlier, the defendant ended up escaping prosecution for sodomy, as the complainant failed to appear in court. However, the defendant was still subjected to scrutiny by the court as a result of the accusation. As Connors (1994, p. 99) reports, "since [the defendant] was a ticket-of-leave holder, the mere allegation of attempted sodomy was damaging and the crown solicitor directed that he be returned to the bench of magistrates to decide the fate of his ticket". A ticket of leave entitled a convict to work and live within a given area before their term had expired, and it also entitled them to own property. This example from the work of Connors again demonstrates how colonial law operated through a particular logic of ownership, whereby it was beneficial for the law to be relatively lenient in granting clemency to white male convicts in order for them to secure ownership of land (even if this was later revoked).

I would also suggest that this logic similarly underpinned the granting of property rights to white women. This is not to negate the campaigns that white women were involved in to win these rights (and later rights to vote and hold office), but that the granting of these rights served a purpose for the white nation: it allowed more white people access to landownership, and thus encouraged an investment in such ownership on the terms set by the white nation (which was anxious to refute Indigenous sovereignty). Implicit to the granting of such rights was the presumption of a nominal heterosexuality for white women. As a result, the invisibility of white homosexual women within colonial law (as opposed to the relative visibility of white homosexual men) was largely due to the equation of the category 'homosexual' with 'homosexual men'. This failure to 'see' white homosexual women within colonial law suggests to me the centrality placed upon the reification of a normative gender order that whilst potentially according a space to white homosexual men (albeit as 'pathological others'), was unable to accord a similar space to white homosexual women. The recognition of such a space would potentially have required a recognition of the anxieties that shape white heteropatriarchy, founded as it is upon the disavowal of white women's sexuality (Stoler, 1995).

The contradictory applications of the law described above (whereby white men were at times convicted of sodomy, but at the same time they were granted clemency in the form of a ticket of leave, or were allowed to maintain property rights following conviction) can be reconciled if viewed as constructing a range of 'aspirational practices'. These practices served to reinforce a series of hierarchies, within which white homosexual men and many white women could gain access to traditionally heteropatriarchal institutions. Such aspirational practices not only outlined for white homosexual men how to access certain privileges, but also directed the white heterosexual majority as how to 'stay white' (i.e., how to maintain their privileges). This racialisation of property rights thus encouraged all white people to adopt normative white values in relation to ownership, and to do so via the disavowal of Indigenous sovereignty. The central understanding of power that informed colonisation was thus a "discourse of [white] sovereignty in which the fact of domination is hidden in a language of legitimate rights" (Stoler, 1995, p. 64). The challenging or repealing of sodomy laws and the ongoing challenges by white queers to gain 'equality' thus implicitly contain reference to what is effectively white queer equality with the unmarked white majority. This logic continues to inform queer rights movements in Australia.

Chapter Summary

Throughout this chapter I have elaborated an understanding of how current understandings of white queer identities *as individual practices* are largely the product of the ways in which white queer experiences have been framed by the law. My concern has been to show that despite ongoing campaigns to deny rights to queer people, and to position queer people as pathological or deviant, white queers continue to benefit from a legal system in Australia that is premised upon the fiction of Terra Nullius, and from a range of social institutions that enshrine the privilege of white people above all others.

I have also sought to elaborate the ways in which gender continues to shape the access that queer people enjoy to state sanction. As I have suggested, white men who have in various ways been identified or seen as queer have enjoyed considerable privileges that have at times been denied to white queer women, and most of the time to non-white queer men and women. My intention has not been to ignore the prohibitions on homosexual practices or identities, but rather to examine how such prohibitions were often tempered by a desire on the part of the white nation to secure landownership and possession in the face of Indigenous sovereignty.

This historical examination of queer identities will, I hope, demonstrate to the reader the importance of the subsequent chapters, which explore in greater detail how particular identity claims are made in regards to white queer rights, and the problems with such claims as they fail to interrogate race privilege. Keeping in mind the multiple relations that white queer men and women have had, and continue to have, to the state will be of importance when considering the following chapters, and will help to illuminate how it is that the race privilege held by white queers continues to operate in the service of the white nation.

☙ 3 Injured Identities

In this chapter I explore what it means to use particular identity claims in the service of rights within the context of a postcolonising nation such as Australia, where such claims to rights are premised upon a notion of loss or injury. Drawing on the work of Wendy Brown (1995), I examine what it means to claim an identity as a white queer person, when that identity is founded upon a notion of personal harm in order to warrant certain rights. Brown suggests that:

> Much of the progressive political agenda in recent years has been concerned not with democratizing power but with distributing goods, and especially with pressuring the state to buttress the rights and increase the entitlements of the socially vulnerable or disadvantaged.... Without disputing the importance of such projects, especially in a political economy fundamentally impervious to human, ecological, and aesthetic life, the dream of democracy–that humans might govern themselves by governing together–is difficult to discern in the proliferation of such claims to rights, protections, regulations, and entitlements. (p. 5)

This statement offers us great insight into the problems that arise when rights campaigns focus primarily on providing redress for wrongs experienced. Not only do such campaigns produce a "proliferation of... claims to rights, protections, regulations, and entitlements", but they also located those who claim such rights in a particular position as individuals who in some way have been 'injured' or hurt by laws or practices that deny their rights as human beings. Of course neither Brown nor myself wish to dispute *per se* the fact that such injuries happen, nor that they are detrimental to the lives of those who experience injury. Rather, our concern is with the political implications that arise from claiming such an injured identity, particularly for those of us who identify or who are identified as white.

In order to elaborate these points, I begin by examining how rights claims based on injury primarily focus on interpersonal rather than institutional forms of violence, and that in doing so such claims paradoxically evidence a desire on the part of white queers to be located within a universal rather than specific set of rights, where the 'universal' is premised on the norms of whiteness. This is particularly the case where queer rights activists make use of the rhetoric of 'human rights'. Such rhetoric, whilst widely used to legitimise rights campaigns, largely ignores how discourses of human rights prioritise liberal individual accounts of subjectivity. In the first section of this chapter I thus begin the work of elaborating the concerns I expressed in the preface in regards to the need for accountability in the use of psychological knowledge in the service of queer rights, and I return to this point in both a later section and in the following chapter.

I then go on to demonstrate some of the problems that arise when queer rights claims are premised upon notions of harm or loss. In so doing I focus on some of the ways in which an injured or 'minority' identity has been claimed recently by (nominally heterosexual) white people both in the US and in Australia, and I suggest that such claims are often played out in the form of nationalist rhetoric that white queers may unintentionally buy into when pushing for rights based upon injury or loss. I conclude by suggesting that there is a largely unrecognised gap between gaining rights that appear to provide protection from injury, and actual changes to social inequity. My suggestion here is that rights claims made by white queers that are founded on a form of 'injured identity' actually demonstrate the investments that white queers have in particular forms of state sanction.

Psychology, Human Rights and Liberal Individualism

There now exists a considerable body of literature that successfully demonstrates the limitations of human rights claims and their call for 'universal values' (e.g., Chesterman, 1998; Harding, 2005; Offord, 2003; Wright, 2001). This literature explicitly challenges what Chesterman terms the "globalising violence of universalism"

(p. 98). We may see such violence at work when particular understandings of subjectivity are privileged within human rights claims. The primary model of subjectivity that informs human rights discourse presumes that we identify ourselves as individuals to the exclusion of all others–that we stand as autonomous individuals rather than as individuals who are thoroughly enmeshed in particular cultural and historical contexts. Whilst this model of subjectivity may have some degree of generalisability within Western nations, it may be of little relevance when applied in countries that have little use for such an understanding of subjectivity.

As such, when this model of subjectivity is employed within human rights discourse to elaborate a *universal* set of claims to rights, it may effectively serve to discount the experiences of self that arise from cultures that may not prioritise individualised accounts of subjectivity. Thus as Chesterman suggests: "Human rights as the constitution of subjectivity is an important part of the urge to bring the Other into 'Western' discourse" (p. 109). Thus, even though such acts of 'globalising violence' have been challenged by those positioned or located outside of the West, and whilst there continue to be calls to reformulate human rights so as to recognise particular contexts and histories, the rhetoric of human rights continues to be used in ways that prioritise the values of Western cultures.

As I suggested in the preface, one of my areas of inquiry in this book is how the social sciences have become intimately involved in rights advocacy. In particular, I am interested in how the discipline of psychology is often used to warrant certain claims to rights. This point of inquiry is of particular relevance to my examination of human rights, as psychological arguments are increasingly being used as 'evidence' in human rights claims. Whilst it cannot be denied that it is a vast improvement to see the discipline of psychology being used in support of rights for queer people (as opposed to psychological knowledge being used in the service of oppression, as I will elaborate in the following chapter), there is nonetheless a pressing need to explore the specific assumptions that are brought to bear upon rights claims when framed through the discipline of psychology.

As many readers may already be aware, the majority of psychological approaches to understanding subjectivity typically focus on the autonomous individual. As such, psychological research predominantly understands subjectivity as intra- rather than inter-subjective. As a result, the locus for change within psychology is taken to be the individual, rather than the social, a fact that allows social injustice at the institutional level to go largely unnoticed due to an individualised focus (Gergen & Walter, 1998). Whilst I will spend considerable time elaborating this point in the final chapter of this book, it is important to signal here that there is most often little space within the discipline of psychology for an understanding of subjectivity that conceptualises identities *as social practices*, rather than seeing identities as the possession of individuals who live in social contexts. This distinction is important as the latter understanding of identity cannot help but see differing subject positions (e.g., those associated with race, gender and sexuality) as operating discretely *within* individuals. As I will elaborate in Chapter Four, this results in a particular form of identity politics that brings with it certain moral standpoints that may at times be antithetical to the development of an ethical framework through which white queers can claim rights.

This focus on a liberal individual understanding of identity—both within the discipline of psychology and within the rhetoric of queer rights activists who draw upon psychological and human rights discourse—produces rights claims that whilst seemingly being premised upon the needs of individual queer people, may instead be seen as implicitly calling for a universal set of rights that primarily reflect the needs of white queers. As such, individual claims to rights by white queer people are reliant upon a form of state sanction that recognises the rights of this particular group of queer people *as white people* to claim a location within the globalising space that is claimed by white hegemony. As I will elaborate in the following section, claims to universality as they appear in the rhetoric of those who may be loosely termed 'white supremacists' are disturbingly similar to those made by white queer rights activists who claim to be disenfranchised from the state.

Discourses of White Injury

In an oft-cited paper in the field of critical whiteness studies, Robyn Wiegman (1999) explores how there has been a turn in the past decade or more towards white people in the US claiming a disenfranchised location. This is the product of any number of historical changes in the US, but has largely come about as a result of the state sanctioning of multiculturalism, subsequent changes in the racial mix of the US (where the US census bureau predicts that by 2050 white people will not be the dominant race in the US), the changing of laws (such as those around segregation and the subsequent introduction of affirmative action), and the investments that certain white people may hold in depicting themselves as differentially 'injured' through their relations to the nation.

Wiegman (1999) cites one particular example where a white person employed the logic of being 'injured' by the law as a result of their racial affiliations/identity in order to claim a particular right. Wiegman reports that:

> In Laurens, South Carolina, John Howard has built [a museum, whose] marquee blares, 'The World's Only Klan Museum'. Inside, there are robes, books, Confederate flags, pocket knives, 'White Power' sweatshirts, even T-shirts declaring 'It's a White Thing. You Wouldn't Understand'. When the local authorities denied Howard a business license to sell souvenirs in the Redneck Shop, he threatened to take his case to court. [His lawyer] Suzanne Coe, [claimed that the case] was about civil rights.
>
> In Alabama, the Birmingham Civil Rights Institute is located across from the Sixteenth Street Baptist Church, the site of multiple bombings in the 1960s, including the now famous one that killed four black girls. Inside the museum are replicas and remnants from the period of official segregation: public bathrooms marked 'white' and 'colored', pieces of a yellow school bus, a segregated street scene. In the gift shop, patrons can purchase African American history books, posters, postcards, T-shirts emblazoned with the image of Martin Luther King Jr.
>
> For Howard, as for his civil rights lawyer, the existence of the Alabama museum–and the legal protections that enabled it and other such projects to come into being–establishes the legitimacy of, if not the legal precedent for, the Klan Museum, guaranteeing Howard's right, in his terms, to display pride in being white. So many of the characteristics of U.S. racial discourse in the 1990s are exhibited in Howard's

> story. Most notably, the language of civil rights is mobilized to protect whiteness, which is cast not only as a minority identity but as one injured by the denial of public representation. In asking the apparatus of the nation to adjudicate this 'minority' injury, Howard seeks the universal and hence abstractly disembodied ledger of rights that are understood as part of the promise of democratic citizenship. (pp. 116-117)

This example from Wiegman provides an excellent illustration of how particular dominant group members can be so unable to see their own position of dominance that they are able to lay claim to being discriminated against as a result of their race (or more precisely, in the case of Mr. Howard, discriminated against for 'having pride' in the actions of their race). More importantly, not only are such claims made, but they are at times recognised by the state (as in the case of Mr. Howard, whose 'Klan Museum' continues to be open for business).

Another example of dominant group members claiming an 'injured identity' was evident in the campaign strategy and policies of Pauline Hanson, an Australian member of parliament and leader of the One Nation party. Ms. Hanson founded her party's position on claims to being disenfranchised: she believed that 'hard working' white people such as herself where being divested of power and status as a result of the rights and privileges that she believed were unnecessarily being accorded to Indigenous people and other groups of non-white people within Australia. Her maiden speech to parliament (1996) provides us with an excellent example of how claims such as these are made within the Australian political context.

> Mr Acting Speaker, in making my first speech in this place, I congratulate you in your election and wish to say how proud I am to be here as the Independent member for Oxley. I come here not as a polished politician but as a woman who has had her fair share of life's knocks.
>
> My view on issues is based on commonsense, and my experiences as a mother of four children, as a sole parent, and as a businesswoman running a fish and chip shop. I won the seat of Oxley largely on an issue that has resulted in me being

called a racist. That issue related to my comment that Aboriginals received more benefits than non-Aboriginals.

We now have a situation where a type of reverse racism is applied to mainstream Australians by those who promote political correctness and those who control the various taxpayer funded 'industries' that flourish in our society servicing Aboriginals, multiculturalists and a host of other minority groups...

Present governments are encouraging separatism in Australia by providing opportunities, land, moneys and facilities available only to Aboriginals. Along with millions of Australians, I am fed up to the back teeth with the inequalities that are being promoted by the government and paid for by the taxpayer under the assumption that Aboriginals are the most disadvantaged people in Australia. I do not believe that the colour of one's skin determines whether you are disadvantaged...

This nation is being divided into black and white, and the present system encourages this. I am fed up with being told, 'This is our land'. Well, where the hell do I go? I was born here, and so were my parents and children. I will work beside anyone and they will be my equal but I draw the line when told I must pay and continue to pay for something that happened over 200 years ago. Like most Australians, I worked for my land; no-one gave it to me.

I and most Australians want our immigration policy radically reviewed and that of multiculturalism abolished. I believe we are in danger of being swamped by Asians. Between 1984 and 1995, 40% of all migrants coming into this country were of Asian origin. They have their own culture and religion, form ghettos and do not assimilate. Of course, I will be called racist but, if I can invite whom I want into my home, then I should have the right to have a say in who comes into my country.

In this speech Hanson employs a wide range of rhetorical strategies in order to warrant her position in regards to rights and multiculturalism in Australia. These strategies have been analysed in depth elsewhere (e.g., Grant, 1997; Hill, 1998; Leach,

Stokes & Ward, 2000; Rapley, 1998), but my interest here is in how Hanson claims for herself a disenfranchised identity.

She begins by stating her credentials to claim a position as an 'average person'—"My view on issues is based on commonsense, and my experiences as a mother of four children, as a sole parent, and as a businesswoman running a fish and chip shop". Statements such as these are used by Hanson to claim that she is committed to a 'solid work ethic', that she has 'commonsense' and that she understands how to 'run a business'. Moreover, she positions herself as doing the 'work of the nation' as expected of white heterosexual women—that of literally reproducing the nation (as signified by her statement 'my experiences as a mother of four children'). The implication of these statements is that Hanson is entitled to speak on matters of importance to the Australian nation—that her 'commonsense' approach is one that will be shared by many other people in similar positions.

She then goes on to make her allegations as to how it is that someone who is an 'average person' like herself can be so disenfranchised: it is the result of 'reverse racism', 'political correctness' and 'separatism'. She also states her fears that Australia will be 'swamped by Asians'. Together, these claims are taken as representing legitimate concern for her own identity as a white person in Australia—by implication she is not being treated fairly, her options are being limited, and she is being forced to act in ways that are not of her choice. It is important to note here that not only was the entire One Nation campaign premised upon statements such as these, but it also had a good measure of success, as seen by the fact that a considerable portion of the voting community at that time shared Hanson's opinions. The position being advocated by One Nation was that white Australians constituted a beleaguered minority who needed to be saved.

Yet, at the same time, Hanson's own rhetoric belies this position of injury. Whilst she feels personally affronted by 'reverse racism' and 'political correctness', she also believes that 'if I can invite whom I want into my home, then I should have the right to have a say in who comes into my country'. Here we can see that Hanson not only believes in her right to define who does or does not come into the country, but that she also lays claim to the country as her own—'my country'. In this we can see that at the very moment where white people claim to feel disenfranchised, they do so from a position of power and privilege. That such privilege is denied, ignored or reinstated is, I believe, one and the same thing. To speak out from a position of power in order to claim to be *powerless* is to trade on forms of state sanction that have been put into place historically in order to provide redress for oppression (e.g., affirmative action in the US and land rights and remuneration in Australia). As I will elaborate in the following section, the claiming of 'injured identities' by white queers in Australia thus runs the risk of engaging in similar practices to those of Howard and Hanson outlined above.

Damaged Goods

Before beginning this section, there are two vital points that require elaboration. First, in critiquing the notion of claiming an 'injured identity' in regards to queer rights, I am in no way intending to suggest that queer people do not experience pain on an almost daily basis as a result of discrimination. Talking about this pain, and developing political frameworks through which to address it, is obviously of great importance. I do not believe, however, that talking about the pain we experience, and challenging how discrimination operates, *a priori* requires us to use pain as the basis of our rights claims *per se*. I believe it is more important that our claims to rights as queer people are recognised because we are entitled to such rights as citizens of particular nations, rather than as individually injured people. What is required from this perspective is not the voicing of pain in order to secure rights, but instead a critique of how such pain is caused by social inequity that results from institutions, such as the law, being founded upon heteropatriarchal values. Understanding the pain that queer people face is obviously a primary source of why we may push for rights in the first place, but it does not need to be the language through which we claim such rights.

The second point requiring elaboration pertains to my previous critique of human rights. As a signatory to particular conventions for human rights (as arbitrated by the United Nations), Australia is in principle committed to upholding and providing for the provision of such rights. Yet, as I will discuss further in this chapter, this has not always been the case. There have been numerous instances (in particular in relation to the treatment of Indigenous people and refugees) where Australia has been accused of failing to adhere to its commitment to particular UN conventions. My critique of human rights rhetoric earlier in this chapter was thus not *per se* a critique of the desire for rights on the part of white queer people, but rather a critique of how such rights are understood within a specific individualist, and psychological, framework. My interest in rights in this section more closely pertains to equal rights claims made by queer people in Australia, though it connects to the notion of human rights in the sense that queer rights campaigns (as I will discuss further) do at times draw upon notions of human rights. Thus my discussion pertains primarily to the *rhetoric* of human rights, and the notion of 'universal rights', rather than to the actual principles of specific human rights conventions.

As I have previously suggested, queer rights claims, both historically and in the present, have relied upon using knowledge produced within the social sciences to 'prove' the normality of queer people (Riggs, 2005b; Rogers & Booth, 2004). Such proof has often relied upon the assumption that the construction of queer people as pathological or deviant serves only to injure queer people—it is damaging to our lives and well-being. Whilst there is of course considerable mileage to be gained from using these types of arguments, my suggestion within this chapter is that they may ultimately serve to co-opt queer people into a particular logic of state sanction, whereby it is the state that can 'save' queer people from 'further damage'. Thus as Wendy Brown (1995) suggests in her insightful analysis of rights claims:

> [Any] effort, which strives to establish racism, sexism, and homophobia as morally heinous in the law, and to prosecute its individual perpetrators there, has many of the attributes of what Nietzsche named the politics of *ressentiment:* Developing a righteous critique of power from the perspective of the injured, it delimits a specific site of blame for suffering by constituting sovereign subjects and events as responsible for the 'injury' of social subordination. It fixes the identities of the injured and the injuring as social positions, and... this effort also casts the law in particular and the state more generally as neutral arbiters of injury rather than as themselves invested with the power to injure. (p. 27)

Brown's points have considerable relevance to the ways in which psychological knowledge is used in the service of queer rights campaigns. Of late there has been a great deal of attention paid to queer rights issues by psychological societies, both in Australia and internationally. Yet whilst these represent important examples of psychological knowledge being deployed in the service of rights advocacy for queer people, they may also work to construct queer people as 'injured' subjects in ways that are not necessarily productive. This notion of the 'injured other' has been critiqued by Amina Mama (1995) in her insightful work on the stereotype of the 'wounded negro', a stereotype that was used to legitimate claims for an end to apartheid in the US (amongst other things). Elaborated predominantly within the discipline of psychology, this stereotype depicted African American people as irreparably damaged by the effects of slavery, the upshot being that apartheid should be abolished so as to avoid 'further damage' (see also Richards, 1997). Whilst Mama is of course not suggesting that slavery did not oppress African American people as a whole, nor that apartheid as a social system should not have been abolished, she is suggesting that the stereotype of the 'wounded negro' had long lasting effects in regards to the ways that white people in America understood the experiences of African American people.

Examples of constructions of the 'injured other' in queer rights campaigns appear in the following extract from a press release by the newly formed Coalition for Equality:

> For decades, the Australian Government has consistently forgotten same-sex couples and their families. This means emotional trauma and financial disadvantage in areas as diverse as the Medicare Safety Net, tax and social security benefits, and benefits provided to Defence personnel in same-sex relationships... we continue to urge politicians at both state and federal level to reconsider the implications of the UN's ruling in the case of Mr Edward Young–which found Australia to be in breach of its human rights obligations by denying benefits to the same-sex partner of a war veteran. (Coalition for Equality press release, 2005)

In this extract, queer people are depicted as facing 'emotional trauma' and 'financial disadvantage', and the answer to this is suggested to be that 'politicians at both state and federal level' need to pay heed to these problems. Whilst my point here is not for one moment to deny the oppression that queer people face in Australia, or the need for some form of rights, my concern is as to how such constructions of queer people as 'injured others' can have negative consequences, where we must first prove psychological distress in order to gain access to rights. An example of this appears in the American Psychological Association's (APA, 2004) position statement on same-sex marriage, where one of the specific resolutions states that:

> Discrimination and prejudice based on sexual orientation detrimentally affects psychological, physical, social, and economic well-being.

Statements such as these, alongside those made in the extract above by the Coalition for Equality, may do very little to challenge how oppression operates through state institutions which, whilst perhaps at times granting rights to queer people as a result of persistent lobbying, have on the whole been unwilling to interrogate how heterosexual privilege (alongside white race privilege) is enshrined within the law and within other such state institutions. As I mentioned earlier, a focus on individual prejudice or discrimination based on individual attributes (such as sexuality) does not necessarily translate into a critique of how such prejudice occurs in the context of a society that is structured by certain beliefs about rights and equality. Gaining access to such rights for queer people may thus come at significant cost, one of which being the construction of queer people as damaged, lacking, or otherwise in distress. Thus as Brown (1995) suggests, "while [rights] formally mark personhood, they cannot confer it; while they promise protection from humiliating exposure, they do not deliver it" (p. 127).

In addition to the above points, and the implications of such constructions of the 'injured other' for the rights claims of queer people (especially as they are promoted within the discipline of psychology), there is a second point that I take from the work of Brown (1995). Brown suggests that the naming of a specific site of blame works to individualise accountability, and thus on the whole frees the State and its institutions of responsibility. Queer rights claims within this logic are thus seen as battles to be fought primarily by individual people, rather than through collectives of people (Wright, 2001). Whilst it is of course true that collectives of people (such as in the example of queer rights campaigns) *do* come together to push for rights, such collectives tend to be constituted by individuals seeking to access *individual* rights, rather than seeking to engage in social change that changes the face of how individualism or collectivity is understood (a point that I will return to in the conclusion of this chapter).

There is of course a third point that comes from the work of Brown (1995), and one that highlights some of the problems that arise when white queers attempt to use analogies between racism and heterosexism to push for rights. Examples of this are often subtle, and are implicit in claims such as the following:

> As with every major human rights advance, from the abolition of slavery to allowing women to vote, future generations will look back and wonder how anyone could have opposed such a basic human right... slavery, racism, persecution of religious minorities—all have existed for thousands of years, all have been perpetuated at one time or another by governments and all are now recognised as discrimination. If appeals to the past could be used to perpetuate the marginalisation of disadvantaged groups, there would be no end to injustice. (Australian Marriage Equality, 2005)

Statements such as these, whilst aimed at demonstrating the importance of granting rights to queer people, may be seen to trade on the oppression experienced by other groups of people, who, whilst quite possibly also identifying as queer, have been engaged in struggles for rights that have at times differed quite significantly from those led currently by predominantly white queers. The risks that arise from attempting to equate differing histories of oppression are thus twofold: First, the comparison of oppression based on sexuality and oppression based on race may not necessarily be conducive to maintaining a critical focus on ongoing race privilege and discrimination. In other words, if white queers use legal precedence in regards to racial oppression as a benchmark against which to measure oppression based on sexuality, then this may well serve to ignore the ways in which the privilege that white queers (as white people) experience comes at the expense of Indigenous and other people variously labelled as 'non-white'. Second, the equation of sexual and racial oppression can effectively sideline the overlaps that exist between racial and sexual privilege and oppression (Barnard, 2003). In the context of Australia, for example, this could well work to position oppression based on sexuality at the forefront of human rights issues, which would obviously do little to engage with the unfinished 'Treaty business' that exists in Australia currently (Haggis, 2005; Moreton-Robinson, 2000).

This issue of drawing analogies between sexual and racial oppression is one that I will return to in the following chapter, but it is important to highlight here the complex interactions that I have outlined within this chapter in regards to the claims to injury made by white queers, and those made by white (nominally heterosexual) people more broadly, such John Howard in the US and Pauline Hanson in Australia. In this light, to claim an injured identity in the context of a postcolonising nation that continues to deny Indigenous sovereignty, and where the rights of white people are asserted over all others, may be a difficult and indeed risky line for white queers to take.

Chapter Summary

As I have suggested within this chapter, to claim an injured identity as a white queer person is not without its problems. Particularly troublesome is the reliance upon one form of gaining state sanction that is largely dependent upon liberal individualism as its model of subjectivity, and which focuses on sanction as freedom from injury, rather than as a more radical revisioning of social justice. The product of this type of approach to justice is that only certain groups of people are accorded sanction, and moreover, that this sanction will come at the expense of others.

Whilst human rights discourse certainly has a place in regards to queer rights (specifically in regards to holding current governments accountable for their commitment to particular UN agreements), it is important to be mindful that a *failure* to uphold the values promoted by the UN is fast becoming a hallmark of Western nations such as the US and Australia, who continue to renege on agreements in regards to rights. What this suggests to me is that rights claims (and the identity claims that underpin them) that are premised upon state sanction as it is currently configured may ultimately serve to enshrine, rather than fundamentally challenge, discrimination against queer people. Moreover, such forms of sanction may serve to render white queers complicit with white hegemony. In other words, by buying into the forms of sanction on offer to queer people currently (sanction that primarily privileges the values and needs of white people), there is an attendant risk that very little will be changed in regards to how queer people relate to the state: we will continue to be reliant upon injury as a legitimate way of claiming identity, and we will thus continually be drawn into parallel with other groups of (white) people who seek rights based on notions of injury.

It is thus my contention that it is important to acknowledge that whilst discrimination does indeed cause pain for many queer people, the voicing of such pain in order to gain rights may serve not only to construct queer people as 'damaged', but also to legitimate particular forms of pain. In the context of a postcolonising nation such as Australia, it is most often the case that the voices that we hear are those of white people. Whilst it is not inherently impossible for queer people who do not identify as white to speak of their pain, it is far less often that this happens and that it is heard. Moreover, as examples such as that of the Stolen Generations enquiry have shown us, not only is it the case that both the Australian government and some sections of the white Australian public have at times refused to hear certain stories of pain, but even when they are heard they produce a particular response—one that does not result in an acknowledgment of institutional discrimination, but rather one that attempts to reduce away the pain of marginalised groups through recourse to notions of 'special rights'. Such rights are seen as being especially granted to certain groups of people (for example, in Pauline Hanson's rhetoric in regards to rights for Indigenous people) *in addition* to the rights enjoyed by all other people. This creates a logic whereby those granted rights to address discrimination are seen as getting more than their due, rather than as gaining access to rights that are already enjoyed by majority group members. Gaining rights for queer people on the basis of injury may thus reinforce the notion that certain groups of people (i.e., queer people) get 'special rights' (indeed, this has been an argument against same-sex marriage in the US), rather than seeing queer rights campaigns as being about granting rights to queer people that are automatically granted to heterosexual people. In other words, we should not have to 'prove our pain' in order to be granted rights–those rights should be automatically recognised through an acknowledgment of the ways in which they are inherently denied as a result of the law under heteropatriarchy–it is the law that is lacking, not queer people.

Finally, I would propose that premising rights claims on injury in the context of a nation where the voices of white people are those that are predominantly heard may perpetuate *white* injury as the focus of queer rights. Likewise, the use of injury as a founding argument for rights may result in the voices of individual people being appropriated in the service of rights claims. These are obviously problems that are to some degree intractable, in that we can never be sure as to which voices will be heard, and it is also the case that precluding the very voicing of pain can itself be seen as an act of exclusion. My intention in this chapter has not been to contribute to the silencing of queer pain, but instead to question how such pain may be framed within a context of rights. These are issues that I return to in Chapters Five and Six, and which highlight the importance of questioning identity claims as they are currently configured within queer politics.

ଔ 4 Unearned Moral Authority

In this chapter I explore what Běrubě (2001) has termed 'unearned moral authority'. My concern here is with some of the problems that may arise when white queer rights activists draw upon particular forms of moral authority that may not only be unearned, but which may also impinge upon or appropriate the moral claims made by other groups of people seeking rights. My intent in this chapter is not to suggest that white queer people should not be allowed to make moral claims—indeed I believe that asserting a wide range of queer-specific forms of morality is an important part of the queer project—but I am concerned about what happens when white queer people assert moral claims in which race privilege is not problematised.

This chapter also extends my examination in the previous chapter of how identity claims operate within queer rights rhetoric by exploring the ways in which moral arguments construct particular notions of what it means to be a 'good queer'. In looking at how the identity 'good queer' is constructed, I am concerned to elaborate how such identities prioritise a particular form of politics, and how such a politics may at times be appropriative.

In order to explore these concerns about unearned moral authority, I start by outlining in greater detail why I see this focus as important. I then in the remainder of the chapter investigate three particular loci where we may see moral assumptions at work in the politics of predominantly white queer rights activists. First, I explore how the discipline of psychology has historically (and indeed at times in the present) been involved in the promotion of particular forms of moral judgments against queer people. In so doing, I elaborate upon some of the ideas introduced in the previous chapter in regards to social scientific research and its use in queer rights campaigns. In particular, I question the benefits of utilising psychological arguments that may often reinforce particular normative moral assumptions.

The second area that I focus on is that of same-sex marriage. In so doing I explore some of the problems that arise when white queer activists use analogies to racial apartheid in their campaigns. I propose that, much like the marriage debate itself, advocacy that is informed primarily by the needs of white queers may do very little to challenge how systemic oppression operates in colonial nations. I also suggest that the use of particular moral arguments in the marriage debate require interrogation in regards to the ethical assumptions that they make.

Finally, I explore one particular example of queer rights activism: the *Let's Get Equal* campaign that is currently being run in South Australia. My intent in looking at this campaign is to highlight how particular claims to rights display a range of moral assumptions on behalf of white queer people that do not adequately engage with issues of privilege.

I conclude this chapter by drawing together my points about unearned moral authority, and I view them in the light of a number of key white lesbian feminist critiques of ethics and moral claims. More specifically, I elaborate what it means to claim a particular moral position as a white queer person, and I point towards some specific ways in which white queers may more productively engage in ethical relationships in the context of colonial nations.

The Use of Moral Arguments in (White) Queer Politics

In their critique of feminist psychology, Kitzinger and Perkins (1993) examine the implicit assumption that psychology should not be about morality, and instead suggest that "nonjudgmentalism, uncritical acceptance of everyone's 'right to her own opinion' and the bland 'validation' of everyone's disparate experience does not seem either possible or desirable from a feminist perspective.... Feminism is a *moral* framework; it involves making judgments about right and wrong, good and bad" (p. 17, original emphasis). Whilst I am of course sympathetic with this argument, and have myself written about privileging the moral values that queer people may differentially hold (Riggs, 2004a), my concern here is in regards to what happens when white queer people ourselves make moral assertions that are taken *a priori* as being true, and thus beyond question.

My point of entry into this line of thinking comes from the work of Bĕrubĕ (2001), in his writings on the 'whiteness' of gay cultures. He suggests that white gay men often lay claim to an 'unearned moral authority' as a result of our experiences of discrimination. This is summed up well by his use of a quote from James Baldwin:

> I think white gay people feel cheated because they were born, in principle, into a society in which they were supposed to be safe. The anomaly of their sexuality puts them in danger, unexpectedly. (p. 256)

This says a great deal to me about the use of moral authority by white queers in campaigns for equal rights: it demonstrates our potential ignorance of unearned race privilege. In other words, maintaining outrage at heterosexism (however justified) may do very little to recognise the relationship that *white queer people* are in to racism simply as a result of *being white people*. Thus as Bĕrubĕ suggests, "gay visibility successes at times exploited and reinforced a racialized class divide that continues to tear our nation apart, including our lesbian and gay communities" (p. 235). By continuing to prioritise the values of white, often middle-class lesbians and gay men in our equal rights rhetoric, we contribute to the ongoing oppression of non-white lesbians and gay men, and to the silencing of other queer people (such as bisexual, transgender and intersex people, as well as those in polyamorous relationships to name but a few) of all colours.

My suggestion here is thus that whilst there is indeed a great need to talk about and prioritise the moral values held by queer people, these values should not be beyond challenge, nor should they without question be the values held by white queers (Riggs, 2006a). This suggests to me that there is a great need to examine the moral claims made by white queers, and to understand the implications of these claims for queer rights in regards to race and race privilege. Otherwise, as Bernard (2003) suggests, "no matter how coalitional its compass, [any rights campaign] that identifies itself in terms of gender and/or sexual orientation only… will be a white-centered and white-dominated politics, since only white people... can afford to see their race as unmarked, as an irrelevant or subordinate category of analysis" (p. 3).

These are of course difficult statements to make in the context of countries such as Australia, the US and the UK, where right wing politicians and media moguls seem intent upon denying queer rights. In-house squabbling over morality, particularly in regards to race (or more precisely, race privilege), may be seen by many as antithetical to claiming queer rights: how can 'we' present a 'unified front' if 'we' can't get over our own differences? This is, however, not something that I would see as the best starting place for engaging in queer politics, nor is it something that will necessarily move us any great distance away from the normative moral assumptions that have often been imposed upon queer people (as I will elaborate in the following section).

Psychology, Morality and Identity Politics

As I suggested in the preface to this book, and as I highlighted in the previous chapter, the discipline of psychology, and the social sciences more broadly, continue to play an important role in defining how non-heterosexual identities are understood and represented. Whilst my interest in this book is to counter notions of a 'queer identity', and to explore how the reification of sexuality as an *a priori* category may well work in the disservice of queer rights, there is still I believe a need to understand how social scientific knowledge circulates in and around queer rights campaigns. In this section I explore some of the normative moral assumptions that are often promoted within the discipline of psychology, and I outline some of the implications of this for the types of identity politics that have at times informed queer rights.

It will no doubt already be obvious to many that psychology has a long history of being involved in particular practices that have been oppressive to queer people. Some of these include: the incarceration of queer people and the application of electroconvulsive therapy, extreme behaviour modification techniques (such as the simultaneous presentation of images of naked men and the administration of an emetic to gay men), and in some cases, psychosurgery such as lobotomies (Terry, 1999). Of course, most practitioners would be right in telling us that on the whole this no longer happens, and that the discipline of psychology is far more enlightened. Whilst this may well be the case, however, I do not believe that this necessarily means that the moral assumptions about same-sex attraction that informed the use of such techniques have changed. In other words, and in psychological talk, the behaviour may have changed, but the thoughts that gave rise to such behaviours may well remain the same.

It is relatively easy for the discipline of psychology as a whole to state that it has examined its moral values or that it is now more liberal in its views. Indeed, it is relatively easy (though the activists who campaigned for homosexuality to be removed from the *Diagnostic and Statistical Manual of Psychological Disorders* may not agree with me) for the discipline in general to *say* that it does not hold biased views against queer people. But it is another thing entirely to have actually interrogated those views, been honest about what they have done in the service of oppression, and to have examined how such views indeed continue to exist (for example, in the field of 'reparative therapy', as I will outline below). There are, I believe, numerous examples of how psychology continues to be complicit with moral arguments that are used to deny the rights of queer people, some of which I will now elaborate.

First, psychology can still be used against queer people precisely because the discipline has quite a visible history of being involved in classifying queer people as pathological (every second paper on psychology and queer experience will cite that 'it was only as recently as 1973 that the APA saw fit to recognise that homosexuality does not constitute a disorder *per se*'). No amount of support for same-sex marriage rights, positive representation in journals, or acknowledgment of the validity of queer experience in the present can undo how the discipline at large has worked against the interests of queer people in the past. We may see examples of this where the Christian Right continues to use the moral authority of psychological knowledge to justify its position that homosexuality constitutes a pathology. Whilst the discipline of psychology may no longer support this position on the whole, there is still a wealth of psychological research that *does* support this position, and which can be used against queer people.

Second, some branches of psychology (though many consider them to be very distant and much poorer cousins) continue to engage in practices that are oppressive to queer people. Indeed, many would suggest that these types of practices are on the rise, particularly within the US, where 'conversion' or 'reparative therapies' continue to be promoted as a 'cure' for same-sex attraction. In claiming 'scientific validity' for their findings, proponents of such therapies use the authority of psychological knowledge to warrant their actions (Riggs, 2004b).

Finally, psychological research most often continues to operate from a particular moral viewpoint on the lives of people who identify as queer. This may range from outright assumptions about associations between being queer and mental health problems (Rogers & Booth, 2004), to more implicit assumptions about how to engage in research with queer communities. Some examples may help illustrate this point. A great deal of 'positive' research on lesbian and gay parents currently continues to compare such parents with heterosexual parents. The moral assumption implicit in this is that there is a useful commensurability between these groups, or that lesbian and gay parents should compare ourselves to heterosexual parents as though this were the standard of excellence that we should aim to achieve (Clarke, 2000; 2002; Riggs, 2005b). This of course represents a moral position that reflects heterosexual values surrounding parenting, rather than necessarily valuing the positions of lesbian and gay parents ourselves.

Another example of moral assumptions being made in research on queer people appeared in a recent publication by Michelle Crossley (2004), who caused a furore when her article on the topic of barebacking appeared in a relatively prominent psychological journal (see papers in Langdridge, 2005, for a commentary on this). Her writing on this topic as a heterosexual woman was not the cause for concern *per se*, but rather that within the article she made a range of moral judgments about gay men who bareback that *were neither explicitly acknowledged as such or warranted in her work*. For example, she depicts barebacking as "self-defeating, damaging and even suicidal" (p. 242), and she suggests that 'gay men's sexual liberation' demonstrates "the latent psychological and social problems associated with [it]" (p. 230). Whilst Crossley in many ways claimed to come out in support of the decisions that gay men make, and whilst Crossley has in the past been at the forefront of critical psychological research on health (e.g., Crossley, 2000), her claims were undermined by the moral assumptions that appeared to inform her work.

From these few examples we may see that both mainstream and more critical approaches to psychology, whilst admittedly showing considerable recent commitment to challenging its members to examine their own prejudice (for example, in the release of press statements by the American, British and Australian Psychological Associations/Societies in support of varying forms of queer rights, or in the publication of articles on commentaries that challenge *individual* prejudice), has not on the whole done so by looking at the moral judgments that continue to shape the discipline (Riggs & Choi, 2006). Indeed, psychological knowledge is often still implicitly represented in many ways as being freestanding from the moral assumptions that circulate in the cultural context within which it is located. Whilst certain more critical sections of the discipline have of course challenged this notion, in my reading there still continues to be a lack of engagement with the moral values held by the discipline of psychology as a whole (rather than just in particular 'critical' pockets of the discipline).

From this brief explication of some of the moral assumptions that inhere to the discipline of psychology, it is possible to see some of the problems that arise when moral frameworks are used as the parameters through which to view the experiences of queer people. As I suggested in the introduction to this chapter, this has led queer people to elaborate our own forms of morality. Yet whilst this is an important tool for validating queer experiences, it is also important that this is accompanied by a critical examination of how particular 'queer moralities' may serve to reify normative accounts of morality, and in particular in relation to the ways in which such accounts understand the concept of 'identity'.

Primarily, psychological accounts of 'the individual' presume an additive model, whereby individual people are presumed to experience discrimination based on sexuality *plus* discrimination based on race *plus* discrimination based on age, etcetera. This understanding of identity promotes a form of essentialism that fails to understand how these 'axes' are interrelated, and correspondingly, how they may operate simultaneously to grant privilege.

This additive approach to understanding identity is also common to what has been termed 'identity politics', where rights movements are organised around a singular aspect of identity (e.g., lesbian/gay rights). Whilst such approaches to activism have achieved a great deal over recent decades, they may ultimately fall short of examining how systemic oppression operates, and may do little to explore alternate ways of claiming rights or identities. In this regard, Harris (1995) proposes that:

> The result of essentialism is to reduce the lives of people who experience multiple forms of oppression to addition problems: 'racism + sexism = straight black women's experience', or 'racism + sexism + homophobia = black lesbian experience'. Thus, in an essentialist world, black women's experiences will always be forcibly fragmented before being subjected to analysis, as those who are 'only interested in race' and those who are 'only interested in gender' take their separate slices of our lives. (p. 255)

Barnard (2003) provides an excellent elaboration of Harris' point about understanding identities as simultaneous sites of difference, rather than as mere 'problems of addition', where he suggests that:

> In the United States... many contemporary political and theoretical formulations of communitarian subjectivity assume that every identity is merely the accretion of so many other base identities (thus, in popular liberal parlance, a Chicana lesbian is said to be triply oppressed as a women, a Chicana, and a lesbian), a paradigm that denies the specificity of identity and the inseparability of the supposed constituents of a particular identity (Chicana lesbian might be an identity in itself, rather than a conglomeration of other identities). Consequently, this paradigm normalizes the modes of subjectivity privileged by material power relations in a particular cultural-historical moment (to compute Chicana lesbian as the sum of Chicana, women, and lesbian, it to establish heterosexual male Chicanoness, white heterosexual femaleness, and white male gayness as the central identities from which the Chicana lesbian draws her constituent parts) and thus erases the experience of those who occupy more than one of the canonized subject positions. (p. 3)

This quote highlights how a compartmentalised understanding of identity (particularly as interpreted within a framework of identity politics) can in effect result in the perpetuation of particular forms of marginalisation. Barnard demonstrates how singular identity politics not only fragment the experiences of particular same-sex attracted individuals (as Harris, 1995, suggests), but also fail to adequately explore how some same-sex attracted individuals (namely those of us who identify as white and middle-class) may experience considerable privilege at the same time as we experience oppression (Riggs, 2006b).

A second problem that arises from singular identity politics, as was highlighted in the quote from Barnard (2003) earlier in this chapter, is that particular issues raised by white queers may not hold the same degree of importance to queer people who do not identify as white (Ahmed, 2004; Weston, 1991). As I will discuss in the following section, the example of same-sex marriage rights has often been the province of white middle-class lesbians and gay men, a fact that requires considerable attention in relation to its implications for activism (Bernstein, 2001). What I will signal here, however, is that it is important to think about what queer people might be trying to gain by seeking state sanction in the form of marriage rights. Whilst many advocacy groups have drawn attention to the considerable gains that may result from accessing marriage rights, it may also be the case that there are other ways of achieving such gains. Indeed, for many same-sex attracted individuals, using state sanction of our relationships as a means to gaining rights may be quite antithetical to our own politics or family forms (Riggs, forthcoming; Weston, 1991).

In summary, then, identity politics have held an important place in challenging normative assumptions surrounding 'queer identities'. Such politics have helped to put queer issues on the public agenda, and have raised awareness of discrimination against queer people. But, at the same time, such politics have introduced a particular (and I would suggest limited) understanding of sexuality and sexual politics, by focusing on singular aspects of identity, and indeed by reifying the concepts of both sexuality and identity themselves. I would suggest that this often leads to the normalising of particular moral standpoints, the outcome being that identity politics as they inform rights campaigns may do very little to shift the terms of debates over queer issues from a focus solely on discrimination, to one that focuses on the simultaneity of privilege and oppression. As I will elaborate in the following section, this is particularly the case in debates over same-sex marriage, which often take as their starting point a range of worryingly normative moral positions in regards to identity, privilege and relationality.

Privilege, Oppression and the Same-Sex Marriage Debate

In an early paper on debates over same-sex marriage, Paula Ettelbrick (1989) suggested that whilst for many same-sex attracted people access to marriage may represent a significant gain in regards to rights, there is little possibility that gaining such access will actually change the institution of marriage in any significant way. It is most likely that heterosexual marriage will continue to be held up as the gold standard against which all relationships are measured, the outcome being that certain individuals and relationships will still be denied state sanction (e.g., those in polyamorous relationships; see Barker, 2004). The problem that arises, then, from an approach to activism that accepts the terms for belonging as defined in relation to particular norms (especially those surrounding liberal individualism), is that queer people are encouraged to accept the incursion of the state upon our lives. Furthermore, those of us who identify as white middle-class lesbians or gay men may well earn rights to marriage that potentially come at the expense of groups of people who are differentially disenfranchised from state sanction.

For example, and as I alluded to in the previous section, the push for same-sex marriage rights is often an issue that is of primary concern to white lesbians and gay men (see also Bernstein, 2001; Ettelbrick, 1998; Riggs, 2004c). Whilst marriage rights may also be of concern to lesbians and gay men who do not identify as white, there continue to be debates within non-white communities (and particularly within African American communities) over the role that same-sex marriage rights would play in combating *racial* oppression. Whilst some of these critiques have been made by African American people who are affiliated with right-wing religious groups, it is nonetheless the case that many people who do not identify as white (but who do identify as queer) continue to question the primacy accorded to same-sex marriage advocacy. As I will elaborate further in this section, challenges such as those raised by African American people in regards to what is often in effect a white queer rights agenda, hold important implications for the moral claims that white queer people make in regards to marriage rights.

One particular example of how queer political organising can often in practice be *white* queer political organising took place in the form of the Millennium March, an event held in Washington in 2000. In an interview between Kim Diehl and Barbara Smith (2000), Smith, a member of the Combahee River Collective, outlines how the event demonstrated the ways in which race privilege functions within what are purported to be 'inclusive' and 'diverse' queer events. Smith suggests that the event was primarily shaped by the needs of white queers, as reflected in a focus on single-issue politics, and in a failure to adequately consult during initial planning of the event, rather than as an afterthought aimed at claiming diversity in representation. Smith also calls into question the rhetoric of human rights that circulated around the event, and the direction of such rhetoric by white queers. Smith's account of the event highlights the very complex ways in which race privilege functions within queer communities, and the importance of examining the complicity of white queers with white hegemony.

Points such as these in regards to race privilege thus demonstrate how the category of queer itself operates in exclusionary ways. In her work on the cultural politics of emotion, Ahmed (2004, p. 148) utilises the metaphor of "sinking into a comfortable chair" to illustrate how the normative status of heterosexuality operates. She suggests that cultural spaces are shaped around heterosexuality, so that, for example, we see billboards featuring heterosexual couples, we see heterosexual couples walking down the street together holding hands, and we hear music and see movies that depict heterosexual lives. This results in public spaces being 'comfortable' for heterosexual individuals.

Importantly, however, whilst public spaces continue to be 'heterosexualised', queer rights campaigns have also sought to promote visibility and awareness, the result being that certain public spaces are 'queered'–they are reshaped to represent the experiences and values of (particular) queer people (for example, think of the large gay communities in San Francisco, Pride events and marches that 'reclaim the streets', alongside representations of queer identities in television programmes). Yet, whilst such reshapings continue to create a public space for (some) queer people, they may also unintentionally perpetuate the exclusion of other groups of people who are not accorded space (e.g., queer non-white people, white transgendered or intersexed individuals, or those white queers who identify as bisexual or polyamorous etc.). Certain 'queer identities' thus gain privileges that may well come at the expense of others, or which may curtail the rights claims of other groups of people (Riggs, 2006b).

Issues of privilege and recognition thus draw attention again to the problems that I previously outlined in regards to single-axis identity politics. As I have outlined elsewhere (Riggs, 2006b; Riggs & Riggs, 2004; Riggs & Walker, 2006), engaging in forms of activism that privilege any singular form of oppression (e.g., sexuality) may well fail to adequately explore how ongoing histories of oppression shape the ways we conceptualise rights. One example of this is in relation to the rights claims of individuals who identify as transgendered, and the overlaps and disjunctures of transgender rights claims with lesbian and gay rights claims. Coombs (2001) suggests that the conflation of 'same-sex attraction' with the category 'gay' (for example) can effectively exclude the experiences of individuals who identify as transgendered (see also Hegarty & Chase, 2005, in regards to intersex activism). The challenge that transgenderism presents to the law (in regards to post-operative legal identification and its relationship to marriage) unsettles the homo-hetero binary in ways that lesbian or gay marriage may not. Thus the push for same-sex marriage rights, primarily by white lesbians and gay men, must necessarily engage with these disparities, and the challenges that they present to any use of identity politics.

In order to further explicate these points about how privilege functions within queer communities, and how this relates to my previous discussion of morality, I now provide a brief exploration of one particular example of how a primary focus on discrimination in regards to sexuality by white queer activists can result in race privilege being ignored. In the particular examples that I examine, racial discrimination is in some ways conflated or compared to discrimination on the basis of sexuality. My interest here is not to depict the research that I focus on as being (a) representative of all white queer writing on same-sex marriage, (b) morally bereft, or (c) entirely, rather than specifically, problematic. Rather, my interest is in how moral authority is warranted within some of the current research on marriage rights, and how this may reflect a particularly white queer position on such rights.

I should also point out here that my argument below in regards to analogies between racial and sexual discrimination is in no way remotely connected to arguments being made in some quarters about the futility of these comparisons on a biological level (e.g., see Throckmorton, 2003). My concern in the analysis that follows has nothing to do with the facticity (or otherwise) of such comparisons, but rather relates to the politics of making such claims, and what they may tell us about the operations of queer white privilege.

It is also important to reiterate here the points that I have made throughout this book thus far in regards to the category 'queer' and its gendered status. As my dear friend Victoria Clarke reminded me recently, whilst it is often the case that lesbian feminists are depicted as holding positions of power from which they seek to 'rule the world', it is far from the lived reality of this group of women, who are often marginalised within academia, denied custody of their children, belittled by the media and heterosexual feminists alike, and routinely ignored in regards to the key challenges that they present to heteropatriarchy. The category ' lesbian feminist' thus continues to be wielded against women who identify with this identity position, in order to deny the validity of their arguments. In the analysis that follows I am thus mindful of how I position the white lesbian authors of the research that I examine. Whilst my intention is to problematise the moral claims that are made by these particular authors, my desire is by no means to ignore the oppression that lesbians of any racial group continue to face in societies that devalue women's experiences in general, and lesbian's experiences specifically.

At the same time, however, I am concerned to draw attention to the ways in which race privilege operates in the relationships between *white* lesbian feminists and feminists (lesbian or otherwise) who are not identified as white. As debates over knowledge claims, and the right to speak for or represent others have shown us, categories such as '(white) feminist' or '(white) lesbian feminist' do not mitigate against the continued enactment of white privilege (Moreton-Robinson, 2000). Indeed, in debates over representation within Australia, white feminists (some of whom identify as radical lesbians) have made claims against Indigenous women in order to deny the legitimacy of their knowledge claims. In particular, this has involved depicting Indigenous women as holding positions of power through which they can deny white feminists job opportunities or career advancement (see Moreton-Robinson, 2000, for an extensive analysis of these issues). Thus whilst I am mindful of the gendered nature of the extracts that I analyse below, I am also mindful of how claims to 'gender solidarity' or coalitionalism have been used to deny the voices of Indigenous women in Australia, and to position Indigenous women as holding power over white women. These are issues that must therefore continue to inform how we understand claims to queer representation and rights. Likewise, it is important that categories such as 'lesbian feminist' are acknowledged as being always already racialised as well as gendered and sexualised.

The following extracts are from two papers written by Celia Kitzinger and Sue Wilkinson, a married lesbian couple who are widely recognized as leaders in the field of lesbian and gay psychology, and have been prominent advocates for human rights. The two papers examined here represent a small part of a large body of research that focuses on same-sex marriage–a body of research that is explicitly grounded in the authors' fight for acknowledgment of their own marriage. My interest here, as I have already indicated, is not in relation to debates over same-sex marriage *per se*, but rather in how such debates are often shaped through the often unacknowledged privilege that white queer people (or in this instance white lesbians) hold.

> Exclusion from marriage – on grounds of the partners' gender, sexual orientation, race, ethnicity or religion – has always been used as a tool of oppression. On 15 September 1935, the Nazis passed the Nuremberg Law for the Protection of German Blood and German Honour stating that:
>
>> Marriages between Jews and nationals of German or kindred blood are forbidden. Marriages concluded in defiance of this law are void, even if, for the purposes of evading this law, they are concluded abroad (Nuremberg Law, 1935).
>
> Likewise, the Immorality Act and the Prohibition of Mixed Marriage Act of the South African Apartheid regime (repealed in 1985) prohibited marriage and sexual contact between

'races'. Forty US states once prohibited 'interracial marriages'... 'Interracial' marriage was still criminalized in 15 US states as recently as 1967, when the US Supreme Court overturned those laws in *Loving v. Virginia*. The parallel with objections to same sex marriage are self-evident. It is this history of marriage that is evoked by Egale, the Canadian LGBT campaigning organization, when it points out that:

> Registered partnerships are no substitute for equal marriage. Imagine if the federal government prohibited interracial couples or Jewish couples from marrying, but said we'll let you register your partnership instead. The very idea is offensive and demeaning. (Egale, 2003)

We believe that no civil institution should be reserved for heterosexuals only, any more than it should be reserved for whites or for 'Aryans' only...

The segregationist 'separate but equal' doctrine was rejected by the US Supreme Court in the *Brown v. Board of Education* case (1954). It ruled that the segregation of schools on the basis of race violated Constitutional equality guarantees, even though the physical facilities and other 'tangible' factors may have been equal. The Court held that 'separate educational facilities are inherently unequal' because to separate students 'from others of similar age and qualifications solely because of their race generates a feeling of inferiority as to their status in the community that may affect their hearts and minds in a way unlikely ever to be undone' (Egale, n.d.). In parallel fashion, the exclusion of same-sex couples from marriage sends a negative message about our status in the community, and humiliates and degrades lesbians and gays – whether or not we personally want to get married, whether or not we personally *feel* humiliated, and whatever our attitudes and judgements about marriage as an institution. It wasn't necessary to approve of the education system to argue for equal entry for black children. It wasn't necessary to approve of the party political system to demand votes for women. It isn't necessary to support the capitalist organization of labour relations to campaign for equal opportunity for women in the workforce. And it is not necessary either to approve of marriage or to want it for ourselves to understand that our exclusion from it is devastatingly unjust. It is, then, in part on the basis of this human rights argument that we support the international campaign for same-sex marriage. (Kitzinger & Wilkinson, 2004a, pp. 133-35).

The arguments in favour of equal marriage in South Africa – a country with a long history of racial discrimination – are particularly instructive. In July 2004 the Lesbian and Gay Equality Project filed an application in the Johannesburg High Court challenging the laws that prevent two people of the same sex from entering into a legally recognised marriage, and in November 2004 the South African Supreme Court of Appeal declared that the common law definition of marriage must be changed to include partners of the same sex. The government appealed, but in December 2005 the Constitutional Court ruled in favour of marriage equality and gave parliament one year to make the necessary legislative changes. Black lesbian activists, including Wendy Isaack, Co-ordinator of the Legal Advice Centre of the Lesbian and Gay Equality Project in Johannesburg make explicit links between the racist oppression of the segregationist apartheid policy and the heterosexist oppression of the segregationist civil partnership policy (Wilkinson & Kitzinger, 2006, p. 55).

These two extracts provide us with a very interesting picture of how moral claims are used in the service of human rights claims, and how such claims evidence the warranting of moral authority on the part of the white lesbian authors that may at times be unearned. Moral claims, particularly as understood through a philosophical lens, are concerned with what is considered to be right and wrong. To speak about one's own morality is to speak about what one believes to be both ethical and unethical ways of relating to other people. The long list of human rights violations that the authors list (e.g., the Nuremberg Law, apartheid in South Africa, segregation in the school system in the US) are in this sense used as a list of wrongs against which to compare the 'wrongness' of denying marriage rights to queer people (my term, not theirs), and thus to implicitly suggest what would be morally right – the recognition that queer people are entitled to access state-sanctioned marriage. Thus whilst their argument is primarily framed in terms of human rights, there is nonetheless a moral imperative that stems from their argument, and one that draws upon the 'moral wrongness' of racial discrimination.

Not only are moral claims implicit to the above extracts, but they are also explicitly voiced in order to warrant the truth claims of the authors. Not only are we led through an account of various forms of racial discrimination as it has been codified within the laws of a range of countries, but we are also shown that what is depicted as 'morally right' has won out in the end – all of the laws mentioned have in some way or another been repealed or overturned. Yet what this argument fails to acknowledge is that whilst this may well be the case, it does not necessarily mean that racial discrimination has been significantly reduced, nor that members of oppressed racial groups have reaped the benefits of changing laws. Whilst no one would deny that the status of non-white people in the countries mentioned above is better now than it was one hundred years ago, it is nonetheless the case that non-white people continue to be over-represented in predictors of poor life expectancy, crime rates, poor health and general socio-economic hardship. Yet, as the authors suggest in the remainder of the paper from which the first extract was taken (Kitzinger & Wilkinson, 2004a), their marriage in Canada afforded them 120 rights at the cost of only $170, many of which they have already put to good use. This, I would suggest, is because the authors already hold considerable privilege as white people (as I do myself), and the addition of marriage as a lesbian couple enforces, and indeed props up, that privilege. In other words, and in contrast to the effects of desegregation and the end of apartheid, two white queer people who are able to access the institution of marriage can quite safely assume that access to said institution will further ensure the considerable cultural capital they already hold *as white people,* rather than the institution bestowing symbolic equality that changes little in the day-to-day lives of those who gain rights (as, for example, in regards to desegregation in the US). My suggestion here is not to perpetuate the 'injured other' stereotype of non-white people, as outlined in Chapter Three, but rather to speak honestly about the limitations of challenges to racial discrimination in Western nations, and to contrast this with the very concrete *and* symbolic benefits that may be gained by white queer people. Access to rights for disenfranchised groups, whether that be for 'black children' or 'working women' (as the authors outline), will always be tempered by the ways in which discourses of race and gender continue to circulate in oppressive ways, *despite* the granting of rights. To believe that acknowledging 'black children's' rights to an 'equal entry to the education system' actually results in this occurring is to ignore how race continues to shape the lives of all people living in Western nations – either to oppress or to privilege.

In addition to the ways in which the authors make moral claims that effectively ignore their own race privilege, they also draw upon the moral claims of non-white queer people in order to warrant their own moral positions. We can see this in the second extract, where the authors refer to the work of "black lesbian activists, including Wendy Isaack". This reference is used to bolster the authors' claim that analogies between discrimination based on race and discrimination based on sexuality are legitimate. The authors thus cite Isaack in order to 'prove' the legitimacy of their claims. This produces an account whereby the authors are in effect drawing upon the moral positions of black queer people in order to warrant their moral positions as white lesbians. Moral authority in this sense is seen as being applicable across contexts, and as transferable between racially diverse populations. Such an approach, however, does not pay significant attention to the incommensurable differences that may shape both the lives of white and black LGBTI activists, and the differences between the political contexts of apartheid South Africa, Jim Crow US, and contemporary UK (where the white lesbian authors are currently located). My suggestion is thus that whilst it is one thing for 'black lesbian activists' to talk about the similarities between racial and sexual apartheid, it is another thing entirely for white queer activists to do the same thing–it requires in part a claim to (unearned) moral authority that in my view seriously undermines the truth claims of white queer activists.

These types of argument (where white people draw upon the moral authority of black people in order to warrant their position) only appear to make sense if we are to accept the authors' representations of the category 'black lesbian activist'. In other words, we are asked to accept that this is a largely representative category, and that people such as Wendy Issack are but one of a vast majority of people who share a similar position. Of course it is no doubt true *in South Africa* that many black lesbian activists may well share Isaack's position, but this does not mean that black lesbian activists (amongst others) living outside of South Africa will share this position. Press releases by the National Black Justice

Coalition in the US, for example, have demonstrated that African American people, queer and straight, hold a range of opinions in regards to marriage, and that some African American people explicitly challenge analogies between racial and sexual oppression. Whilst, as I mentioned earlier, some of these statements have been made by African American people who are leaders of right-wing religious groups, it is nonetheless the case that the warranting of white queer moral authority through the appropriation of the voices of non-white people only appears coherent when the voices of non-white people are represented as unified rather than diverse. What is missing from these types of arguments, then, are the complexities of privilege and oppression that circulate *simultaneously* around the rights claims of white queer people.

On the whole, the white lesbian authors of the above extracts make explicit and implicit moral claims about what it means to be a 'good queer person'–those who fall into this category will recognise the inherent wrongness of certain laws, will draw out the relevant analogies, and will thus automatically come down on the side of queer rights. In the paper from which the first extract was taken (Kitzinger & Wilkinson, 2004a), the authors outline a 'pragmatic argument' for their marriage. Whilst, at a personal level, this argument makes a great deal of sense, if we are to locate it within a broader set of cultural discourses where white hegemony continues to function through particular state institutions, then an argument for white queer marriage becomes somewhat less about pragmatism, and somewhat more about privilege. Thus whilst the two authors appear at times to recognise that they are indeed making moral arguments, there appears to be little engagement with the implications for making these arguments *as white queers*.

My interest in this section has not been to suggest that these particular authors should not make moral claims, nor that the moral claims they make are implicitly wrong. Rather, my interest has been to look at how moral authority is warranted by white queers (or in this instance a married white lesbian couple), and how this authority may come as a result of the appropriation of the moral positions of queer people who do not identify as white, and through a failure to interrogate white queer privilege. As I will explore further in the following section, a failure on the part of white queer people to explore the implications of our moral claims can result in queer rights campaigns being premised upon a desire for rights that, whilst potentially benefiting all queer people, may still inherently benefit certain queers over others.

Who Is the 'Us' That Is Getting Equal?

In this section of the chapter I explore one particular example of how queer rights campaigns in Australia have at times ignored the racialised nature of their claims, and have therefore failed to examine the differential access that Indigenous queers (amongst others) may have to the rights that are currently under contestation. My particular concerns are with the moral implications that arise from claims to equality that do not interrogate racism and race privilege. In other words, my question in this section relates to how queer rights claims evoke a particular moral stance in regards to the 'wrongness' of inequality in the face of the law (what I referred to in the previous chapter as 'injury'), and yet how this wrongness may be perpetuated if queer rights campaigns do not acknowledge how the law is not only sexualised and gendered, but also racialised.

The *Let's Get Equal* campaign in South Australia represents itself as "a lobby group for equal rights for same sex couples" (2004). Though the campaign embodies an important intervention into heterosexist practices in state policy, it fails to recognise the racialised nature of the law itself, and thus also fails to do so in the particular amendments that it recommends. Some of the examples of legislation identified in conjunction with the Equal Opportunity Commission as discriminatory include the fact that

> If you are in a same sex relationship, unlike married or heterosexual de facto couples,
>
> - You will not inherit your partner's assets if they die without a Will.
> - You will pay expensive stamp duty if transferring property between yourselves.
> - If your relationship ends, you cannot access cheap court assistance to disentangle finances and divide property.

- You are not entitled to be paid compensation for the grief you suffer if your partner is killed as a result of a criminal injury.
- You may be denied access to your sick partner if they are hospitalised. You may be denied access any information about their condition.
- You cannot access assisted reproductive technologies.

Whilst the contestation of these discriminatory practices is important work, it is not located within a framework that acknowledges Indigenous sovereignty as the ground upon which we live in Australia, nor does it pay significant attention to the ways in which the logic of 'equality' primarily refers to the equality of white queers with white heterosexual people. Thus, for example, questions of 'assets' and 'property' are rendered problematic if we are to examine them through the lens of racialised ownership in Australia (Moreton-Robinson, 2004a; Riggs, 2004c). For many Indigenous queer people, property ownership, or indeed access to the means to owning property (i.e., a secure job, lack of financial debt, support from financial institutions), may well be mediated by racialised assumptions. It would be erroneous to believe that an Indigenous gay man and a white gay man (for example) would be given equal standing when applying for a home loan, or approaching a real estate agent.

The focus on questions of 'assets' and 'property' also fails to recognise that white queers who do have such privileges do so as a result of the benefits that result from ongoing histories of dispossession. Seeking equality in regards to property does not challenge white 'ownership', nor does it draw attention to the ways in which race impacts upon socio-economic status (tied as it is to 'assets' and 'property').

The assumptions about 'criminal injury' and 'hospitalisation' that appear in the list provided by the *Let's Get Equal* campaign are also mediated by race. The evidence presented in the 1991 Aboriginal Deaths in Custody report highlighted the fact that Indigenous people are disproportionately incarcerated for allegedly 'criminal activities', and that *a priori* assumptions about 'Indigenous guilt' often come to bear upon the outcomes of court cases. Similarly, access to hospitalisation is mediated both by the accessibility of hospitals for Indigenous people living in remote regions, and also by the racism that Indigenous people often encounter in (white-run) hospitals. Thus the base issue here for Indigenous queer people may not be solely about whether they can access 'compensation' or 'sick partners', but rather how the legal and medical professions have worked against the rights of Indigenous people in regards to justice and health care.

Similarly, assumptions about 'criminal injury' and 'hospitalisation' do not give explicit attention in the campaign to discourses of race. Thus the campaign fails to recognise that states of health and illness in Australia are directly related to ongoing histories of colonisation. The vast disparities between white and Indigenous health in Australia demonstrate the fact that whilst white queers may be "denied access to [a] sick partner if they are hospitalised", we have a far greater likelihood of enjoying good health in general, which is in direct contrast with all the statistics on Indigenous health. The ability of white queers to enjoy such good health is a result of our privileged access to health care services that are designed for, and run by, white people. The campaign does not draw out these disparities in any way.

Finally, issues surrounding reproductive technologies have received considerable attention within the media. Many white queer activists have called upon discourses of 'human rights' in order to justify access for lesbians and gay men (e.g., Kitzinger & Wilkinson, 2004b). Yet, recent analyses of human rights discourses (e.g., Harding, 2005; Riggs & Walker, 2006) have suggested that such discourses may be of little use to queer people in fighting for access to reproductive technologies, as they are reliant upon the interpretative judgment of the law. Moreover, recourse to notions of 'human rights' again ignore the racialised nature of the category 'human', and the attendant presumptions which often normalise the values and experiences of white men and women.

In this regard, Indigenous and African American scholars (e.g., hooks, 1981; Moreton-Robinson, 2000) have long drawn attention to the fact that at the same time as white women have advocated the 'right to choose' whether or not to get pregnant or to carry through with a pregnancy, Indigenous and African American women have been fighting against involuntary sterilisation and the removal of their children. In addition to the fact that Indigenous women have had to fight against sterilisation and the forced removal of their children, Steinberg (1997) points out that access to reproductive technologies, even in the light of human rights claims, are still mediated by economics *in conjunction with race*. Thus many Indigenous queer people seeking to access reproductive technologies may not be able to do so even if the laws were changed–their socio-economic status may well prevent access to these costly procedures. This is of course not to deny that many white lesbians (in particular) are denied access to reproductive technologies, nor to suggest that all Indigenous queer people will not be able to afford reproductive technologies, but rather to highlight the differential ways in which race impacts upon access to such technologies for queer people.

As this brief analysis of the *Let's Get Equal* campaign shows, fighting for 'equal rights' may well render white queers complicit with the logic of the law under white heteropatriarchy, in that it ignores the racialised nature of the law, and thus fails to acknowledge how race mediates access to economic, social and political privilege (Lipsitz, 1998; Moreton-Robinson, 2004a; Riggs, 2004c). It is indeed the case, as Matthew Loader (2004), a gay white spokesperson for the *Let's Get Equal* campaign suggests, that:

> It is axiomatic for any poststructuralist that language is a site of power. Terminology and the wording of legal definitions must be accommodating of relationship diversity and consistent with our model of hierarchy-less equality. It goes without saying that terminology must in particular be gender neutral.

It is also the case, however, that any critique of terminology must similarly examine the racialised nature of language and its everyday use, and that such an examination must be wary of the ways in which claims to neutrality can effectively contribute to the invisibilisation of racialised oppression. Thus as Rea Saunders (in Gays and Lesbians Aboriginal Alliance, 1994), writing as an Indigenous lesbian, suggests:

> I feel that coalition politics is important, but first we need to have an understanding and acceptance of differences. We have to confront honestly our own racism, sexism, homophobia and classism and acknowledge the differences between us. Only then can we work together towards a real sense of coalition. Coalition politics can only be effective if people in-

volved are on an equal level. I mean, I am not interested in coalition politics where men still run things. (pp. 7-8)

In order to more honestly engage with a praxis of queer rights in the context of Indigenous sovereignty, those of us who identify as white queers must critically examine the moral claims that we make in regards to rights, and how our 'equal rights' campaigns may only serve to prop up the institutions of white heteropatriarchy: changing heterosexist laws does not automatically mean critiquing race privilege (Stoler, 1995).

Towards a Reflexive Queer Ethics

In this final section of the chapter I draw upon the work of white lesbian feminists in order to sketch out one shape that a queer ethics in the context of a postcolonising nation such as Australia could take. I take as my starting point two possibly contradictory quotes that I believe signal two of the key strands of thought that require attention in regards to any form of queer ethics, particularly as elaborated by white queers. The first comes from Margaret Urban Walker (1992), who suggests that:

> The recent feminist challenge to the legitimacy of moral philosophizing… requires that any ethics done must become politically self-conscious and reflexively critical, and that the impetus to this must be *right in* the kind of ethics any of us do, not an addendum or postscript to it. (p. 24, original emphasis)

The second comes from Marilyn Frye (1990), who Walker discusses in her own paper. Frye suggests that:

> My intuition is that the need for an ethics is race, class and history specific. It is a need felt by people with an investment of a certain sort in being good and/or in others' being good, in doing the right thing, being right, or being in the right. Not everyone at every time has such an investment. (p. 133)

The quote from Frye echoes my own concerns mentioned in an earlier section of this chapter, where I suggested that white queer people are at times invested in constructing particular types of 'good queers', and in outlining what it means to be on the side of moral good. Thus as Frye suggests, the very need for moral positions is almost certainly a desire specific to certain contexts, and to the lives of particular people. This suggests to me that at certain times and for particular people there is a great deal to be gained by claiming moral authority. Claiming to be 'acting from good' can allow certain groups of people to assert the validity of their truth claims, and it can afford certain groups of people the moral high ground. This of course is not inherently problematic. I am most certainly making a moral argument of sorts in this book–that queer rights requires accountability in regards to race and race privilege. What I think the quote from Walker suggests, and in accordance with her argument that there is a necessary distinction to be made between theories of morality and a project of ethics, is that it is possible to speak about queer ethics without them necessarily being totalistic or prescriptive.

Where Frye's (1990) argument is at its strongest is in her suggestion that the use of moral claims to warrant a 'good queer identity' is most typically the province of those who hold the privilege necessary to do so. Moral claims require not only a particular stand on morality, but also in practice require a place from which to speak them *and to expect them to be heard*. To claim the moral high ground is thus often an action achieved by those accorded the right to speak–in this instance, white queers. When those of us who identify as white speak out in regards to rights, and assert that we are entitled to do so, we draw upon our privilege as white people living in a society that accords us significant social status, *regardless of our sexuality*.

What this suggests to me, along the lines of Walker's (1992) statement, is that white queers may speak of ethics *only if* we do so through a critically reflexive lens–if we take our primary ethical obligation as being the need to be accountable for our privilege, and from that starting place to elaborate how we may claim rights *on the contingency of that initial recognition*. This would also require a recognition of the potential for incommensurability in regards to moral positions. In other words, differing queer claims to ethical positions may be inherently incompatible–it may be neither possible nor desirable to reconcile the needs of white queers and non-white queers, or indeed those of white queers and non-white heterosexual people.

Walker (1992) proposes that one way of developing a form of ethics that does not accord hegemony to any particular group would require a 'logic of interpersonal acknowledgment'. Whilst this is certainly an admirable goal, there is a pressing need, as Rea Saunders (in Gays and Lesbians Aboriginal Alliance, 1994) suggested in an earlier quote, to examine our differences, and to not reduce these differences to identities, but rather to look at the differences as social practices that accord privilege or reinforce oppression. Otherwise, there is a great risk involved in claiming that there can be 'interpersonal acknowledgement' in the context of postcolonising nations such as Australia, where the sovereignty of Indigenous people as First Nations people is not recognised. Such a risk comes when certain groups of people are accorded recognition as speaking subjects (i.e., white queers), whilst other groups of people are not recognised as speaking subjects at all.

Chapter Summary

As Allan Bĕrubĕ (2001) has suggested, white queers often lay claim to an 'unearned moral authority'. Thus as James Baldwin stated in a quote earlier in this chapter, those of us who identify as white queers are often so focused on the heterosexist violence that we encounter in our lives that we fail to examine our location within racialised hierarchies. Thus our use of moral authority in campaigns for equality often demonstrates our ignorance of unearned race privilege: maintaining our outrage at heterosexism does very little to recognise our relationship to Indigenous sovereignty (cf. Riggs & Riggs, 2004). By continuing to prioritise the values of white, often middle-class lesbians and gay men in our equal rights rhetoric, we contribute to the ongoing oppression of many differing groups of people differentially disenfranchised from state sanction.

I have proposed in this chapter that in order to speak out from an ethical position, those of us who identify as white queers living in Australia need to work with from an explicit acknowledgment of race privilege in order to develop grounds from which to challenge the mutual operations of racism and heterosexism. If we continue to leave the normative position of our whiteness unexamined, then our moral authority remains complicit with white heteropatriarchy. By examining our own moral claims, and by looking at what we can bring to a coalition with Indigenous people, those of us who identify as white queers may more reflexively engage with multiple *simultaneous* axes of privilege and oppression, rather than simply focusing on our sexuality (Riggs & Choi, 2006).

My proposal here is thus relatively simple: yes, we need to be talking about morality, yes, we need to look at how certain moral judgments (such as those at times promoted by the discipline of psychology) have been used against queer people, and yes, we need some form of greater rights for queer people. But I do not believe that these three affirmatives must preclude an examination of race privilege within queer politics, nor do I believe that they need to lead to the reassertion of yet another set of moral judgments based on the presumed to be norms of queer cultures. To me, to speak of morality is to look at precisely how moral values work to oppress, to discriminate and to perpetuate violence against marginalised groups. This I believe could constitute one ethical starting place for examining moral values within queer rights advocacy, rather than getting involved in yet more liberal blanket statements that don't contribute to a shift in the dynamics of racialised and sexualised power as they are configured under white heteropatriarchy.

⍟ 5 What's Love Got to Do with It?

In this chapter I extend my arguments made in the previous two chapters in regards to identity by examining what it means to claim state sanction based on (a) a particular notion of what it means to be a 'good queer', and (b) the reification of sanction as referring to particular white understandings of subjectivity. Drawing on the work of Sara Ahmed (2003), Luce Irigaray (2002) and Judith Butler (2004), I provide an account of the limitations that arise when state sanction is taken as being the be all and end all of queer rights.

In order to elaborate these issues, I focus in this chapter on the slogan 'Love makes a family', a phrase that has been recently employed in a number of (predominantly white) queer parenting rights campaigns. Such campaigns draw on a discourse of love to demonstrate that queer parents love their children in much the same way that heterosexual parents love their children. Whilst it is presumed that this will be an important counter to constructions of queer parents as pathological, my suggestion is that it may do very little to actually examine how discourses of love work in the service of the white nation, and how they may render those of us who identify as white queer parents complicit with white violence against non-white people (in particular Indigenous people and those people positioned as 'enemies of the nation'). This I believe is an important analytic move, as it has been far too easy for those of us who identify with this subject position to presume that our marginalised position in regards to sexuality somehow locates us outside white privilege (see also Barnard, 2004; Bĕrubĕ, 2001).

In the sections that follow I elaborate how discourses of love in regards to the slogan 'Love makes a family' hinge upon particular understandings of parenting and families. By examining how such discourses of love may work in the (dis)service of white queer parenting rights, I suggest that rights campaigns must do more than simply push for legislation that recognises the rights of queer people who are taken to be always already white and middle-class. They must also occur in a context whereby we examine how citizenship and belonging is constructed in Australia upon the disavowal of Indigenous sovereignty, and through the construction of certain people as being enemies of the white nation. I will propose that these types of disavowal demonstrate some of the ways in which a desire on the part of some queer people in Australia to be acknowledged or recognised as citizens with particular rights may be seen to render queer rights campaigns complicit with the new forms of Empire that are being played out in post-colonising nations.

My intention in analysing the slogan 'Love makes a family' is not to suggest that 'love' doesn't have a place in queer families, but rather that love as a 'turning towards another' may constitute part of the work of understanding how power operates through privilege, and what this may mean for white queers living in Australia. Such an approach would not locate those of us who identify as white queers outside of white hegemony, but rather may allow for an ethical engagement with love that recognises its inherent ambivalence as constitutive of possibilities in the context of a 'post-colonising nation'.

The Object of Love

> Privileging the use of verbs which take a direct object encourages the subject-object relation to the detriment of the subject-subject relation, which needs a little more indirection in order to avoid the reduction of the other to an object of one's own... "I love to you" is more unusual than "I love you", but respects the two more: I love to who you are, to what you do, without reducing you to an object of my love. (Irigaray, 2002, p. 60)

In her recent work on love, Luce Irigaray highlights the problems that arise within the English language as a result of its predominant focus on substantive meaning. This focus on the substantive produces a logic whereby language is assumed to represent the literal interpretation of objects, rather than understanding language as an always inadequate tool for interpreting ourselves and our experiences. This literalisation of language is evident in the slogan 'Love makes a family', which produces a very particular form of love that is rendered intelligible within a substantive framework. More specifically, the 'love' in 'love makes a family' is accorded a functional role, where it is understood to be productive of the category family. Love thus becomes something that: (a) is done to us (i.e., we are 'loved' into a family), (b) is formative of who we are, or are not (i.e., those of us in families are 'loved'), (c) excludes certain forms of family (i.e., those that are not 'all about love'), and (d) produces a realm of intelligibility within which subjects are acted upon as objects (i.e., 'love' is an agency that is directed towards or upon us). One outcome of this is that when we talk of 'love making a family' we are directed into making a series of substantive assumptions that promote certain family forms over others, and which construct 'love' as an action that is all encompassing. The implicit directive is that a 'real' or 'good' family will know that it is constituted through love–that the meaning of love or its value within a family is unequivocal.

One of the problems that arise from rights campaigns organised around the slogan 'Love makes a family' is that the endorsement of love becomes an organising principle for political action. Yet, following Sara Ahmed, we may ask the question: "How has politics become a struggle over who has the right to name themselves acting in love?" (2003, p. 1). Ahmed's question challenges us to look at what the naming or claiming of love may achieve in relation to politics. Moreover, it questions which types of love are allowed, and which types of love are disavowed. If, as common knowledge tells us, queer people have historically been constituted as engaging in forms of love that are prohibited, or which are actively depicted as immoral or pathological, then surely any political rhetoric that highlights 'love' as the central motif will potentially work in the service of those who would seek to perpetuate the disavowal of queer people. It would be naïve to think that simply by claiming to be acting 'out of love' that queer parents will be accorded rights. Thus as Phelan (2001) suggests: "Appeals to [lesbian] maternal love and examples of happy families will continually confront the fear that these parents' love will lead their children to accept that which should not be accepted. Maternal love then becomes not domesticating and instructive, but seductive" (p. 64). Such fear is often evidenced when public opinion is solicited in relation to legislation over lesbian and gay rights. For example, in relation to same-sex marriage rights in the US, one heterosexual respondent stated that

> Contrary to some opinions, love does not make a family. Love, certainly, is one component of a healthy family, but to say that love makes a family places the well-being of children into the hands of subjective emotions and standards. I would offer, instead, that based on centuries of experience and valid research, that only when a man and woman lovingly commit to a lifetime of fidelity, responsibility and hard work are the best interests of children and society served. (Finn, 2002, p. 2)

Here it is proposed that the statement 'Love makes a family' must be measured against 'valid research', which takes as central the role of 'man and woman' in constituting 'valid' (rather than 'subjective') love. Here again the substantive function of the slogan 'Love makes a family' works against lesbian and gay parents to deny that we can adequately 'do' the type of love that is required to constitute a family.

Phelan's (2001) point above in regards to seduction also demonstrates an important consideration in regards to the gendered nature of discourses of love. The stigmatisation and pathologisation of same-sex attraction does not occur in the same ways for queer men and queer women. Whilst this may be an obvious point, there are several implications that result from it in relation to the slogan 'Love makes a family' that may be less obvious. The first of these is the degree of threat that queer female or male bodies present to the patriarchal nation. Queer female bodies (and by association, queer female parents) may challenge the nation through the repudiation of men's control over women, or through the refusal to recognise patriarchy as legitimate. The bodies of queer males (and queer male parents) threaten the hegemony of patriarchy in different ways. Gay men may be seen as undermining patriarchy through a refusal to perform masculinity in particular acceptable ways, or in performing acceptable masculinity within the context of a queer male (read: non-normative) body. Of course, queer men and women may do all or none of the above. My point is that the ways in which the bodies of queer men and women are differentially understood as threats to the nation impacts upon the types of access we are allowed in relation to families and parenting. Whilst, as Phelan suggests above, lesbian mothers may be depicted as seducing their children into an 'unhealthy lifestyle', gay men may be (and indeed are) depicted as physically seducing their children (Riggs, 2004a; 2006c; Rofes, 1998). The gendered nature of parenting, alongside the acceptable forms of maternal and paternal love available under heteropatriarchy, work in conjunction with one another to position queer parents as 'loving inappropriately'. Claiming that 'love makes a family' may thus do very little to destabilise negative portrayals of queer families in regards to normative discourses of familial love.

A final outcome that may result from the use of the slogan 'Love makes a family' is that love becomes primarily functional–it serves to do things. Love in this sense becomes a form of legitimisation, a form of justification, and ultimately I would suggest, a form of domestication. Robson (1992) suggests that lesbian parents become domesticated when certain normative understandings of family and parenting are imposed upon, and accepted by, lesbian parents. The notion that 'love makes a family' is of course not solely the product of queer rights campaigns. The use of love as a rhetorical tool for justifying certain family forms (i.e., the heterosexual nuclear family), and for protecting the rights of certain family members over others (i.e., men over women, parents over children), has long been identified as oppressive (e.g., Pollack & Vaughn, 1987). Taking on board the notion of 'love makes a family' without problematising it or questioning the logic that inheres to it may thus be counterproductive to the aims of lesbian and gay rights campaigns. As I will discuss in the following section, there is also the potential that 'love' as a constitutive discourse of family may work in the service of the white nation, regardless of the sexuality of the parent.

Citizenship and State Sanction

> Moving towards citizenship for sexual minorities will require not just an expansion of some boundaries, but a wholesale re-

thinking of the relations among citizenship, family, masculinity, religion and sexuality. (Phelan, 2001, p. 9)

As the Australian nation continues to be confronted by the fact of Indigenous sovereignty, alongside a recognition of ongoing histories of colonisation and dispossession, there exists a profound uneasiness in relation to white claims to belonging in this country. For some people, this uneasiness is routinely dismissed through recourse to discourses of 'Indigenous violence', or 'the inevitability of progress'. Such discourses seek to justify colonisation and thus discount the histories of white violence that Indigenous narratives demonstrate (Riggs & Augoustinos, 2004). Yet in much the same way, this uneasiness is dismissed by white people who seek to 'right the wrongs', or engage in 'anti-racism'. Claims to benevolence, to 'giving up power', or involvement in 'practical reconciliation' also serve to overwrite Indigenous narratives of violence, or at the very least, to justify white belonging in Australia (Riggs, 2004d). Such claims do not represent a 'turning toward another', but rather demonstrate one of the ways in which a focus solely on "showing the face of the white subject... *sustains the direction or orientation of [the] gaze*, whilst removing the 'detour' provided by the reflection of the other" (original emphasis, Ahmed, 2004, p. 5). In other words, a focus on the 'good things' that white people engaged in anti-racism do, or a discussion of privilege that fails to look at what privilege is founded upon, serves to maintain a focus primarily on white people, without actually examining the relationship that white people are always already in with Indigenous people, amongst others (Nicoll, 2004a).

These points about the disavowal of white violence are also evidenced in the ways in which white queer parents attempt to seek equality with the white heterosexual majority in regards to rights. The claiming of rights by white queers signifies a desire not only to have entitlement to such rights recognised, but also to have the legitimacy of particular queer identities acknowledged as valid forms of citizenship (Phelan, 2001). This desire for an acknowledgment of validity (in addition to the right to civil liberty and protection), whilst understandably representing a desire to live a life free of anti-queer violence, also signifies a desire for acknowledgment within the national imaginary. Such a desire, however, could potentially come at significant cost.

One aspect of this cost would be a committed investment to the terms for belonging as set by the nation. Whilst the nation is composed of a great range of people from a wide range of cultures, the politics, economics and social fabric in Australia is predicated upon 'illegal possession' (Moreton-Robinson, 2003). To seek protection within the nation, and to do so through a desire for an acknowledgment of being, thus requires a taking on board (at least to some degree) of the terms for sanction set by the State (Butler, 2002). This obviously presents a problem to white queers, namely: whose rights and desires take precedence in a postcolonising nation? Should our primary responsibility as white queers be first to an ethical engagement with Indigenous sovereignty, and only then to securing rights for groups of people who are also currently disenfranchised within the national space? Or, as Phelan suggests in the above quote, does a desire for full citizenship on the part of white lesbians and gay men require a radical rethinking of national belonging that would take as its starting point the fact of Indigenous sovereignty, a move that could be productive of a 'queered' national space that begins the important work of rethinking how we understand belonging, families and parenting (Barnard, 2004; Nicoll, 2001)? And of course there is the pressing need to examine what it may mean for a queer Indigenous person who lives within the Australian nation (shaped as it is upon the disavowal of Indigenous sovereignty), and who may well experience an uneasy relationship to queer rights movements, which typically do not allow a space for representations of queer Indigenous people: how is citizenship possible for someone whose life is disavowed in multiple, concurrent ways?

To return to my focus on the slogan 'Love makes a family', the above point about reconfiguring the national space requires that we examine how love has been used to secure the white nation. Ongoing contestations over land rights and native title, and the refutation of them under the current Howard government, represents a form of white violence whereby Indigenous people are positioned as not adequately 'loving the nation'—as knowingly attempting to destabilise the white nation. This, in combination with the ongoing pathologisation of Indigenous families and parenting (as evidenced through the refusal of the Howard government to offer an apology to the Stolen Generations), suggests that we may see how the type(s) of love given sanction within the nation are those that pledge allegiance to a white history of Australia. As Povinelli (2002) suggests, "Love does not make an Indigenous family *qua* traditional family to the Australian Parliament and courts, nor do local notions of corporeality, proximity, affect, place, context, or spirituality" (p. 227). The reification of national love therefore serves to perpetuate the colonisation of Indigenous people's lives by confirming the status of white hegemony in Australia. White queer parents who seek a place within the nation as recognised citizens thus trade on the forms of national love that are currently sanctioned, which are founded upon both the disavowal of Indigenous sovereignty and the construction of other groups of people as enemies of the nation.

What is required here, then, is an understanding of how the use of the slogan 'Love makes a family' by white queer parents works in the service of Empire. Empire building from this perspective becomes a practice of co-option, whereby previously disenfranchised groups (such as white queers) are given space within the national imaginary (albeit on terms highly delineated by the heterosexual majority) in order to reinforce the hegemony of whiteness. This provision of space turns on the reification of particular forms of love, and requires that white queer parents accept the particular 'ideal object' of love that is reinforced by the white nation. Complicity with such practices of Empire thus reveals the contingency of queer rights upon the forms of citizenship already available within colonial nations, rather than necessarily representing a radical repudiation of 'heteronormative citizenship' (Johnson, 2003).

National Loving & 'Good Queers'

> The construction of subordinate identities may sometimes not necessarily take the form of constructing minority plaintiff identities so much as constructing plaintiff identities that still privilege, and indeed in a sense perform, dominant identities–identities that pass. (Johnson, 2002, pp. 327-328)

At this point it may be instructive to return to Irigaray's (2002) questioning of the substantive logic of love-as-having. In her excellent discussion of love and its operations in relation to nationalism,

Sarah Ahmed (2002) elaborates how love-as-having (object directed love) becomes a form of national ownership, whereby the love that we lay claim to reinforces who we are. In other words, when we claim a form of love as our own—when we take an object as being the site of our love—then that love enables us to claim a position within the national ideal in regards to loveable objects. Our love for another thus becomes the love of what another can bring us, or what they represent to us. Love in this sense does not represent a turn towards the other, but rather forecloses the reciprocity that a 'love to another' (in Irigaray's terms) could engender. Love-as-having—love as a symbolic approximation of a national ideal through ownership of the object—may do very little to refuse the types of love that claim hegemony within the nation. Indeed, love as ownership may very well reinforce the types of 'loving belonging' that have informed white belonging in Australia since colonisation.

It is of course important to clarify here the limitations to the above explication of love-as-having in regards to white lesbian and gay parents. Whilst the slogan 'Love makes a family' would appear to demonstrate a certain willingness to commit to the terms for belonging or acknowledgment within the white Australian nation, it must also be recognised that under the current Howard government there are limitations as to how far queer people will be admitted into the national space, regardless of any commitment to a particular white model of state sanction. Carol Johnson (2002) suggests that the terms for queer rights that are set by the nation encourage a form of passing, whereby queer people must be complicit with our own oppression in the form of passing off our relationships as 'just like' heterosexual relationships, and in not being 'too threatening' in our behaviours and words in public spaces. She suggests that this encourages the performance of the subject position 'good queer', where certain non-heterosexual bodies are granted recognition as a result of their ability to look as the nation would desire them to look (i.e., not queer, not threatening, not subversive etc.). In regards to 'Love makes a family' campaigns, the notion of the 'loving (lesbian or gay) family', whilst potentially running the risk for accusations of 'seduction', may also in part conform to the non-threatening image of lesbians and gay parents as being 'just like' heterosexual parents (Clarke & Kitzinger, 2004).

One of the key problems that arises from this location of queer parental love within the terms of a national imaginary (alongside the previously discussed problems of objectification and ownership) is that it is premised upon the exclusion of non-heterosexual families and parenting styles that do not or cannot conform to those deemed acceptable (Phelan, 2001). Thus, for instance, whilst 'Love makes a family' type campaigns may push for the rights of all queer families, it is far less likely that children in families with bisexual or transgendered parents, or where the parenting roles are shared between a wide range of people (e.g., polyamorous relationships) will be recognised as exhibiting legitimate forms of love. This again draws attention to the distinction between access to rights, and acknowledgment of being—whilst some lesbians and gay men may be able to gain acknowledgment of the validity of our relationships within a national imaginary, this may come at the expense of those queer families or relationships that are not accorded acknowledgment (Stoler, 2001).

Furthermore, it is not only the case that white queers are able to claim a space for our love as a result of ongoing colonising violence against Indigenous people (e.g., in regards to the refutation of land rights claims and the refusal to offer an apology or negotiate a treaty). The white nation also reinforces its hegemony by positioning certain groups of people (e.g., asylum seekers) as being enemies of the nation. Whilst of course many white men and women, both heterosexual and queer, do indeed challenge the government's policies on mandatory detention and other forms of human rights violations against asylum seekers, this does not negate the fact that our belonging as white people is further secured through the construction of certain groups of people as enemies. Political and media representations in Australia of the 'children overboard scandal' demonstrate one of the ways in which a position of love is claimed by the white nation through contrast with those positioned as unable to appropriately 'love their children'. In other words, reports of asylum seekers threatening to throw their children overboard in order to be granted asylum (reports which have since been shown to be false) were used by the Howard government to bolster the contrast between white Australians who 'love their children', and asylum seekers who will 'risk their children's lives' (O'Doherty & Augoustinos, 2005). Asylum seekers are thus positioned as threats both to their own children and to the 'national love' of white Australians.

Finally, in a global context, where white/dominant group members maintain such a stranglehold on economies, politics and social welfare, it would be disingenuous to suggest that white queer people in Australia do not stand to benefit from such imbalances in power. As I suggested earlier, whilst there are many white people (queer or otherwise) who challenge particular acts of exclusion or oppression (such as through refusing to shop at multinationals or campaigning for an end to sweat shop labour or petitioning for acknowledgment of human rights violations), this does not change the fact that we continue to live in a social and political climate that both prioritises our voices and opinions, and which continues to afford us privilege. Claiming a position of love in Australia currently is thus extremely tenuous, and whilst it may be true within particular queer households that 'love makes a family', such love is highly contingent upon the contents of a national imaginary that refuses love to many groups of people, and which is founded upon the denial of Indigenous sovereignty.

Loving Other-wise

> We cannot then equate love with justice. Justice is not about learning to love others, let alone loving difference. Justice is not about "getting along", but should preserve the right of others not to enter into relationships, 'to not be with me', in the first place. The other, for example, might not want my grief, let alone my sympathy, or love.... Love is not what will challenge the very power relations that idealisation "supports" in its restriction of ideality to some bodies and not others. In fact "to love the abject" is close to the liberal politics as charity, one that usually makes the loving subject feel better for having loved and given love to someone whom is presumed to be unloved, but which sustains the very relations of power that compels the charitable love to be shown in this way.... In the resistance to speaking *in the name of love*, in the recognition that we do not simply *act out of love*, we can find perhaps a different way of orientating ourselves towards others. (Ahmed, 2003, pp. 44-47, original emphases)

In this section of the chapter, I would like to tentatively sketch out some of the possibilities for 'loving other-wise'. This term, which I take from the work of both Luce Irigaray (2002) and Lorraine Johnson-Riordan (2005), suggests a number of important dimensions of love in the context of a postcolonising nation. Most importantly, this term is *not* intended to suggest a benevolent turn towards the other—that 'all we need is love' to do the work of addressing white violence in Australia. Instead, the term 'loving other-wise' suggests two potentially more productive and honest engagements with an ethics of love in a postcolonising nation. First, there is the need, as Sara Ahmed (2004) suggests, for white people seeking to challenge white privilege to not simply stop at interrogating our own privilege, but that such an examination of privilege must entail a 'turning towards the other'. Such a turn need not be one of benevolence (i.e., to 'help the other'), nor one seeking solace (i.e., 'the other can teach me what to do better'), but rather would constitute a recognition of how white privilege is constituted through its corollary of both Indigenous disadvantage and the construction of some groups of people as 'enemies of the State'. 'Loving other-wise' in this sense may represent a move towards recognising the role that the location of the other plays (and has always played) in the constitution of the white self: the ways in which notions of the 'good white person' have always already been contingent upon constructions of 'the primitive', constructions that, whilst not reflecting the actual location of the other, *do* signify how the (absent) presence of the other is engaged with. This generates questions such as 'what purpose do constructions of "Indigenous threat" (for example) serve the white nation?' rather than questions that seek to look simplistically at either 'what is white privilege?' or 'what are the problems faced by the non-white other?' Whilst understanding white privilege and non-white disadvantage has an important place in challenging the hegemony of whiteness, the notion of being 'wise of the other' may enable us to actually turn towards the other at the same time as we examine white privilege. This may also involve, as Sara Ahmed suggests above, a recognition of the fact that another may not want to enter into a 'loving relationship' with the one who offers love, or that claims to love may be unwelcome in regards to racialised power imbalances.

This brings me to the second implication of the term 'loving other-wise'. This is perhaps a more literal meaning: that there is a need to understand how love is constituted in a network of power relations, 'otherwise' we will fail to see how claims to love may work in the service of white hegemony. This understanding of 'loving other-wise' places a prohibition on blithely continuing the government sponsored agenda for 'practical reconciliation', with the presumption that all that is needed is yet more (white) attention to issues of Indigenous disadvantage. Such a presumption constitutes what Fiona Nicoll (2001, p. 154) has referred to as the difference between 'reconciliation to' ("to make another resigned or contentedly submissive"), and 'reconciliation with' (which "conveys the meaning of 'harmonising', 'healing' or 'making friendly after estrangement'"). The term 'loving other-wise' in this sense is thus a clear signal to those of us who identify as white to begin the work of thinking through how white violence continues to be enacted in the name of the national good (Rutherford, 2002). The term also suggests, again following Ahmed (2003), that attempts by white Australians to engage in 'reconciliation with' Indigenous people may be refused–that the ambivalence of love in a postcolonising nation such as Australia requires that those of us who identify as white must recognise that our desire for 'harmonising' or 'healing' may be neither desired or welcomed by Indigenous people. Recognition of the ground of Indigenous sovereignty as the precursor to any engagement with reconciliation by white people thus allows for the possibility of refusal as an inherent right of Indigenous people who are recognised as knowing subjects. To do anything else would be to yet again fail to understand white identities as constituted through racialised power networks that cannot be sidestepped simply by naming whiteness or 'owning up' to white privilege (Ahmed, 2004).

Whilst an extended discussion of how racialised power acts in the service of subject constitution will be provided in the following chapter (see also Moreton-Robinson, 2000; Riggs & Augoustinos, 2005), it is important to point out here how power as an artefact circulates *between* people in the service of subject constitution (as opposed to the assumption that it operates solely *within* people). Such an understanding of power holds important implications for how we understand 'loving other-wise'. If power is understood as the property of the (white) individual, something that can be taken or given up at will, then power will always remain the property of those who hold hegemony (Moreton-Robinson, 206). Thus the power to tolerate, or to give up power, becomes yet another reinforcement of power itself, rather than an actual engagement with another who may be the object of that power (Hage, 1998; Nicoll, 2001). Power in this sense is evident in the slogan 'Love makes a family', where a substantive logic makes one person an object of another's love. This notion of a one-to-one correspondence between the object of our love and our approximation of a national ideal of love fails to adequately understand how the national ideal circulates as an object that is impossible to have. To have love (to own or posses love) is not the same as *being for* love (Irigaray, 2002), much the same as to lay claim to power is never sufficient enough to actually occupy a site of unequivocal power (Butler, 1997).

Racialised power circulates upon and between bodies, but cannot be pinned down as a property that is held without challenge. Obviously certain (white) bodies lay claim to a position of power, and indeed occupy a site of privilege that is dependent upon the enactment of power, yet such bodies are always constituted in a relationship to historical and spatial forces that are constantly under contestation. To see power as a property solely of particular white bodies (and thus to see other bodies as always without power) is to reinforce the illusion of white sovereignty that has itself been dependent upon a disavowal, rather than an overwriting, of Indigenous sovereignty. Following Hook (2005), we may thus understand this disavowal as having forever changed white claims to power. In other words, the confrontation with the fact of Indigenous sovereignty cannot be simply denied or displaced, but rather the act of disavowal demonstrates that the white subject (and nation) is forever changed by the encounter. Forms of 'national love', and the types of 'love for another' claimed within the rhetoric of government sponsored reconciliation, are examples of the ways in which this encounter is managed.

Chapter Summary

I tell a story about the relations I choose, only to expose, somewhere along the way, the way I am gripped and undone by these very relations. My narrative falters, as it must. Let's face it. We're undone by each other. And if we're not, we're missing something. This seems so clearly the case with grief, but it can be so only because it was already the case with desire. (Butler, 2004, p. 23)

The above points about the ways in which power circulates around discourses of love in postcolonising nations such as Australia demonstrate the ambivalence of love. Love, whether it be for the nation, for another, or as an act of familial constitution, is always contingent in Western (post)colonial nations upon the suppression of its other: hate. This suggests that in order for us to understand how love functions as a nationalist practice (and what this may mean for the slogan 'Love makes a family'), we must look at the location of claims to love within a range of historical frameworks (Stoler, 2001). How do claims to love work to distance us from violence? How does love-as-having serve the purpose of claiming ownership or a right to acknowledgment? And how may the claim to 'act from love' actually enact a violent erasure of those who are taken as an object of this love?

What I have demonstrated in this chapter are some of the problems that may arise from the claim that 'Love makes a family'. Slogans such as these, whilst potentially having some utility in equal rights campaigns, may do very little to challenge white queers to examine our complicity in practices of exclusion, particularly those more subtle forms that work in the service of Empire. Though it may be important to gain access to rights for the sake of our families, and whilst an accompanying acknowledgment of the validity of our family forms may be of vital importance for some queer people, it is important that this does not come at the expense of examining how discourses of love may demonstrate a possessive investment in patriarchal white sovereignty. As I have suggested throughout the past few chapters, rights claims that start from individual queers, and which rely on singular identity politics to make their claims, may not adequately account for ongoing histories of white violence and their role in legitimating white belonging and citizenship.

What would seem to be required, then, is a move towards what Butler (2004) has referred to as the ways in which our relationships with others 'undo us'. Rather than positing that 'loves makes a family', we may instead look at how love 'unmakes' a family, in both negative and positive ways. For example, in regards to negative ways that love 'undoes us', how may discourses of love marginalise particular families, or tear families apart when violence results from claims of love? How may families fall apart when some members refuse to accept the types of love that other family members value? In regards to the potentially positive outcomes of being 'undone by love', we may look at how the deconstruction of discourses of love holds the potential for creating radical understandings of family and kinship (as queer families have long been engaged in, see Weston, 1994): How may the unmaking of particular family forms (specifically, the heterosexual nuclear family) contribute to the destabilisation of heteropatriarchy and result in a concomitant shift in understandings of rights, citizenship and the white nation itself?

These types of questions, which draw attention to the inherent ambivalence of love, demonstrate how we are undone by the relationships we have with other people. This is not only the case for those we are 'in love' with, or those we take as the objects of our love, but also for those with whom our relationships are based less on love and more on fear, resentment or disavowal. We are undone precisely when our claims to love reflect back to us those people we refuse love to, or whose love we designate as invalid. Reflecting on how love operates in the service of hate and exclusion will be an important role for rights campaigns that recognise the need to acknowledge and engage with their complicity with regimes of white terror and new incarnations of Empire.

ଓଃ 6 Possessive Investments

The impetus for this final chapter comes from the challenge presented to white queer people by the fact of Indigenous sovereignty. As Fiona Nicoll (2000) suggests, writing as a white queer woman, "Indigenous sovereignty exists *because* I cannot know of what it consists; my epistemological artillery cannot penetrate it" (p. 370, original emphasis). To write of what Indigenous sovereignty means to those of us who identify as white queers living in Australia is thus not to attempt to *speak for* Indigenous sovereignty, but rather to recognise how it constitutes a fact that is formative of white identities in Australia. In other words, as a nation defined as 'postcolonising', Australia continues to engage in the refutation of Indigenous sovereignty, and continues to claim rights for white people that come at the expense of Indigenous people. Yet, as Nicoll suggests, such rights claims never actually serve to fully overwrite Indigenous sovereignty, nor do they erase Indigenous rights to belonging and ownership. As I will elaborate throughout this chapter, claims to rights by white queers may thus be seen in many ways to render us complicit with what Aileen Moreton-Robinson (2004) refers to as the 'possessive logic of patriarchal white sovereignty'–in pushing for rights, white queers may well affirm our commitment to the terms for belonging set by the white nation.

The 2004 federal election in Australia provided me with one example of how Indigenous rights may at times conflict with or challenge the rights that white queers attempt to claim. This was particularly evident to me in the fact that the Family First party (who promote the belief that "family grows out of heterosexual relationships between men and women") was, at the time of the election, headed by an Indigenous woman, Andrea Mason. This challenged me to question the political implications of this as a white gay man living in Australia. How did Mason's rights as a (nominally heterosexual) Indigenous woman challenge my desire for rights as a white gay man? Moreover, how do Indigenous rights and white queer rights intersect, and what are the implications of this for my research on racism, lesbian and gay parenting and white belonging in Australia?

These questions again came up at a conference on race and whiteness held in Brisbane, Australia, in late 2004. In her keynote address, Aileen Moreton-Robinson (2004b) examined a selection of speeches by Prime Minister John Howard, in which she elaborated how they evidence a 'possessive investment in whiteness'. Moreton-Robinson suggested that not only are Howard's speeches racialised so as to privilege white Australians and our claims to belonging in this country, but they are also sexualised, in that they often explicitly argue for the normative status of heterosexuality, and in particular, the heterosexual nuclear family. Yet, at the same time, Moreton-Robinson suggested that possessive investments may be unwittingly taken up by those who do not identify as heterosexual. Moreton-Robinson's analysis led me to question precisely how Howard's rhetoric may encourage those of us who identify as white lesbians and gay men to buy into the possessive investment that he promotes. In this way, debates over queer rights may be seen as one of the ways in which white queers are encouraged to voice a desire to be accepted as part of the white nation, and thus to reaffirm an investment in the possessive logic of heteropatriarchal white sovereignty.

These two examples of the intersections between Indigenous rights and the rights of white queers demonstrate to me the fact that those of us who identify as white queers need to more adequately theorise our relationship to Indigenous sovereignty, both historically and in the present. This is not to suggest that discrimination or violence against white queers is not real or dangerous, but rather to point towards the fact that our oppression occurs at the same time as our privilege—we cannot simply presume that our call for rights does not impinge upon the rights of Indigenous people, and that the granting of such rights may not serve to prop up the possessive logic of white belonging in Australia.

In order to elaborate these points within this chapter, I start by exploring in greater detail the concept of a 'possessive investment in patriarchal white sovereignty' (Moreton-Robinson, 2004a). This concept, I believe, is immensely powerful for understanding why it is that those of us who identify as white queers may quite unwittingly be complicit with the disavowal of Indigenous sovereignty when we make our rights claims. This, I propose, occurs not simply through a failure to look at our race privilege *per se,* but rather because our very claims to rights are premised upon histories of colonisation and dispossession in Australia. In order to further elaborate this point, I go on to provide a theoretical account of how I see white racial subjectificiation operating in colonial nations such as Australia. This is something I believe to be a crucial tool required for queer rights agendas, and is something that demands attention and interrogation *prior to* the actual voicing of rights claims. I conclude by proposing an approach to rights claims on the part of white queers that could achieve this. I do this not as a form of prescription for how rights claims *must* look, but rather in the spirit of generating critique and engagement over the fact that those of us who identify as white queers "need to acknowledge the ownership of the land we are living, working and playing on" (Converry, cited in Nicoll, 2001, p. 210).

Possessive Investments

> Invisibility is a dangerous and painful condition, and lesbians are not the only people to know it. When those who have power to name and to socially construct reality choose not to see you or hear you, whether you are dark-skinned, old, disabled, female, or speak with a different accent or dialect to theirs, when someone with the authority of a teacher, say, describes the world and you are not in it, there is a moment of psychic disequilibrium, as if you looked into a mirror and saw nothing. (Rich, 1986, p. 199)

> There is nothing promiscuous or even vaguely erotic about [a] vision of gays happily married and corralled behind picket fences, complete with neo-liberal 'aspirations'.... [The] notion of camp can be opposed [to] a 'straight' sensibility defined by the search for 'authenticity': of national identities, of gender, of sexualities and of 'being' itself.... In certain contexts, the values of white heterosexual masculinity could also be embodied by white heterosexual women. (Nicoll, 2004b, pp. 179; 172; 173)

These two quotes, both written by white queer women engaged in the work of anti-racism and anti-heterosexism, demonstrate some of the vastly different critiques of white heteropatriarchy that have been developed over the past two decades. The first, written in the context of the US by Adrienne Rich, elaborates the ways in which lesbians (amongst others) may find themselves written out of particular spaces, when those in positions of dominance choose not to recognise their legitimacy. The second quote, written by Fiona Nicoll in the context of Australia, challenges what I believe to be one of the implications of Rich's statement: that what is needed is for lesbians (for example) to reassert their right to appear 'in the mirror'. In contrast to this suggestion, Nicoll proposes that there exists a certain 'straight sensibility', wherein the 'search for authenticity' may establish a 'vision of gays happily married and corralled behind picket fences'. Whilst I do not believe for one moment that this vision underpins Rich's statement, it is nonetheless the case that her statement in many ways asserts a particularly normative understanding of 'the mirror'. In other words, to assert one's right to appear in the mirror as a white lesbian or gay man may well entail doing so *at the expense of* someone else's rights. To claim authenticity may be to position someone else as being 'inauthentic'. Thus to extend the analogy made by Nicoll, white heterosexual masculinity could also be embodied by white queer people.

In making these statements as a white middle-class gay man, as I have throughout the entirety of this book, I am thoroughly aware of the potential that exists for being read as dismissive of equal rights campaigns. Yet the problem that I think the quote from Nicoll (2004b) draws our attention to is how queer rights are framed, and more particularly, whose interests are being served through queer rights campaigns. The answer to this, I would suggest, is that it is primarily the interests of white queers that are being served. The assumption of a normative whiteness informing queer rights is I believe inherent to the quote from Rich (1986). Indeed, we may read the quote as somehow suggesting that all lesbians are white: if 'lesbians aren't the only people to know' invisibility; if invisibility is *also* known by those who are 'darkskinned' or who 'speak with a different accent or dialect' to the majority, then surely the implication is that we have the category 'lesbian', and then we have the category 'dark skinned', and the two are somehow seen as mutually incompatible. Assumptions such as these in part have directed my points of inquiry throughout this book, and I think that the concept of 'possessive investments' is of great use when attempting to grasp how it is that the word 'queer' in effect becomes 'white queer' in queer rights rhetoric.

Aileen Moreton-Robinson's (2004a) work on the 'possessive logic of patriarchal white sovereignty' suggests three key aspects that demonstrate the investments that *all* white people in Australia have in colonisation. Firstly, she suggests that the possessive logic "works ideologically and discursively to naturalize the nation as a white possession", secondly, that it is "predicated on exclusion and what it does not own–the sovereignty of the Indigenous other", and finally, it "promotes the idea of race neutrality on the premise that 'race' only belongs to the other" (pp. 5-6). In this section I will elaborate some of the implications of these points in regards to white queer claims to belonging in Australia.

As I have suggested through all of the chapters in this book, white queer people may often be involved in claiming rights that are premised upon our race privilege. In other words, queer rights rhetoric may at times work to naturalise rights as something that are the inherent rights of all people, without adequately exploring how rights are actually accorded to particular groups of people according to their relationship to certain social norms. In this sense, being queer does not place white queers outside of whiteness, nor does it stop white queers from benefiting from unearned race privilege. Rather, it points towards the fact that sexuality is always already racialised, and that what is required is an understanding of 'racialised sexuality', rather than continuing to view race and sexuality as separable, and thus differentially applied to individual people.

Of course, and as I suggested in the previous chapter, white queer people will often be accorded a lesser status as a result of social prohibitions on same-sex desire. And it goes without saying that queer experience is always already shaped through social institutions that discriminate against queer people. Sexuality thus does of course mediate access to rights for queer people. But my argument here, particularly when framed by the concept of a 'possessive investment in patriarchal white sovereignty', is that whilst sexuality mediates rights, sexuality is nonetheless always already racialised, and as a result white queer people benefit from race privilege.

It is important to clarify here, however, that my interest is neither to rank forms of oppression, nor necessarily to provide a deterministic account of white queer experience. Rather, my intention in utilising the concept of possessive investments is to focus on how easy it is for white queers to lose sight of our privilege. In other words, racism continues to function to both oppress and privilege, despite the 'best intentions' of white people, queer or otherwise. To challenge the possessive logic is thus to engage with Moreton-Robinson's (2004a) suggestion that such a logic refuses to acknowledge the fact that white people are racialised, and that such a logic is aimed at claiming ownership of Indigenous sovereignty. The development of rights claims by white queer people must therefore respond to the implications of this logic for white queer rights claims.

White Violence and the Fact of Indigenous Sovereignty

To become an intelligible subject within a colonial nation such as Australia is to be formed in relation to a series of norms. The subject of the Australian nation (as distinct from Australian citizens) continues to refer primarily to the white, middle class, heterosexual subject, a subject who is formed in relation to the possessive logic of white ownership. Such investments are structured through the *disavowal* of Indigenous ownership, and are a continuation of the acts of dispossession and genocide that are formative of the Australian national psyche. Hook (2005) usefully distinguishes between denial (understood as the refutation of another's claim or statement, and the subsequent blanking out of the affect associated with the occurrence of that claim) and disavowal (understood as an act of perception that, whilst refuting the knowledge of another's claim, actually evidences the ongoing impact on affect that the claim makes). A fine line, indeed, in distinguishing between denial and disavowal, but one I believe to be useful for understanding how white subjectivities are forever founded (or indeed founder) upon the anxiety that the fact of Indigenous sovereignty produces, whilst at the same time evidencing the ongoing enactment of such anxiety. The term 'disavowal' thus signifies the relationship that white people are always in with Indigenous sovereignty (Nicoll 2004a), and the importance of grasping how this shapes the collective psyche of the white Australian nation.

To unpack this somewhat; the originary violence of the Australian nation continues to shape the ways in which those invested in the white nation relate to one another. It requires that this violence be routinely disavowed, in order to construct a notion of 'the good nation'. Indeed, as Rutherford (2002) has suggested, notions of a 'national good' are intimately related to national violence–the former exists precisely as an enactment of the latter. This results in white people claiming a location as subjects of the Australian nation at the expense of Indigenous people in two ways: (a) as a result of the fact of Indigenous dispossession (i.e., those of us who identify as white claim to belong to land that is stolen), and (b) through the construction of Indigenous people themselves as a threat to the Australian nation, a claim that is used to further exclude Indigenous people from representation within the national space (Riggs & Augoustinos, 2005). In order for these two factors to be rendered normative, the nation requires nominal members (i.e., those who are recognised by the nation as being legitimate subjects of the nation) to invest in the disavowal of Indigenous sovereignty. Here we can see how white queers, whilst not approximating the location of the white subject of the Australian nation in its entirety, remain nonetheless invested in its possessive logic. Whilst we may be differentially recognised as speaking subjects as a result of our sexual practices, we continue to benefit on a daily basis from our nominal relationship to white hegemony.

In return to the aforementioned notion of a 'collective psyche', it is possible to conceive of this term as referring to the collective ways in which *all* white Australians (regardless of sexuality) are invested in maintaining the unequal power relations that exist under colonialism. Colonial power in Australia, and its operation through discourses of racialised difference, work in the service of white hegemony by setting up a series of exclusionary binaries wherein representation is reserved primarily for white people. If white ways of knowing and conceptualising subjectivity are taken as normative in Australia, then by default it will be the case that 'being intelligible' (as a subject of the nation) will only be extended to those who are established through the language of the nation (i.e., one that is founded upon the denial of colonial violence). The collective psyche of the white nation is thus formed in a relationship to racialised practices of power that are performed by recognised colonising subjects who hold an investment in this power. Such enactments of power attempt to exclude Indigenous people from representation by attributing the role of 'object' to Indigenous people. However, such attributions are rarely successful: though the white Australian nation may believe in the success of its psychic power, this success is rarely evidenced as a totality within the nation. Indigenous people have always resisted colonial power, and continue to challenge the hegemony of white ways of knowing. Furthermore, what Moreton-Robinson (2003, p. 31) has termed Indigenous people's "ontological relationship to land" continues to unsettle claims to white belonging by demonstrating the inalienable rights that Indigenous people hold within the land.

Becoming an Intelligible (White) Subject

It may be important to further clarify here what I mean in regards to a 'collective psyche', and the implications of this for my elaboration of white queer 'possessive investments'. As I will elaborate in this section, talking about a 'psychic life' or a 'collective psyche' need not be understood as referring to an internal set of mechanisms held *by* white people. Likewise, talking about a 'psychic life' does not have to be reliant upon liberal individual notions of identity, as I critiqued in Chapters Three and Four. Rather, my point is that white hegemony is secured as a result of white people being invested in race privilege that comes as a result of our location within racialised hierarchies. Colonial power from this reading thus produces a psychic life that reflects the processes through which 'individual white people' are rendered intelligible as racial subjects within particular social contexts. In other words if, as I have previously outlined in regards to the ways in which white people in Australia disavow Indigenous sovereignty, we are to understand a collective psyche as the site where white Australian subjects are made possible within particular contexts, then understanding racism becomes not a matter of individualisation or internalisation (as the opposite of exteriorisation), but rather one of subjectification, where becoming intelligible subjects on the terms set under colonial power requires white Australians to be spoken into existence as subjects through racism. This process requires that the collective psyche held within colonial nations be taken up as an available resource by all nominal members, and actively reiterated and normalised on a daily basis.

There is an important point that I should clarify here, however, in relation to racism as a formative aspect of subjectification in colonial nations. There is a risk that a statement such as this will be read as one which absolves white Australians of responsibility or accountability. In other words, if occupying the site of the subject in Australia means being spoken through discourses of racism, then it could be inferred that white Australians are interpellated into racism, and that this is something that is beyond our control. However, following on from Butler's (1997) critique of the notion of interpellation as outlined in *Psychic Life of Power*, we may understand that subjects are not hailed by a sovereign power that identifies them as racialised *after* their formation as a subject. Thus as Butler suggests:

> The interpellation of the subject through the inaugurative address of state authority presupposes not only that the inculcation of conscience already has taken place, but that conscience, understood as the psychic operation of a regulatory norm, constitutes a specifically psychic and social working of power on which interpellation depends but for which it can give no account. Moreover, the model of power in Althusser's account attributes performative power to the authoritative voice, the voice of sanction, and hence to a notion of language figured as speech. (pp. 5-6)

My suggestion here is thus that the (white) subject of the Australian nation may be understood not as one who is addressed as racialised after its inception, but rather that the very speaking of intelligible national subjects in Australia is founded upon the racialisation of a collective psyche itself. In order to further develop this understanding of how the white subject is raced at the moment of their/our initiation into networks of power, and the implications of this for understanding racialised practices in our everyday lives, I would suggest that what is required is a focus on how particular bodies are 'made to matter'. This, as I will elaborate in the following section, will further demonstrate my claims as to the foundational aspects of racism in Australia, and its relation to subjective investments in whiteness as collective psychic responses to colonial violence.

The 'Epidermilisation' of Difference

In the example of colonisation in Australia, there exists a long history of both colonising authorities and academics theorising (and legislating) over the bodies of Indigenous people—of both using the body of the racialised other to determine access to rights and subjectivity, whilst simultaneously denying the reality of the body in order to justify claims such as those underpinning the fiction of Terra Nullius. In other words, only particular bodies have been constructed as mattering in Australia. The irony of this is that such bodies (i.e., those of white people) have most often not been marked as (racialised) bodies in the eyes of the nation. Thus, as I suggested in the previous section in regards to subjectification, the subject that comes into being under the sign of race is one that is prescribed by the hierarchical forms of knowledge that are deemed intelligible within the framework of race itself—only certain bodies (materialised through visual markers that are accorded value within racialised systems) are ascribed with power, at the expense of those bodies positioned as being without (or unable to have) power.

Racialised differences are thus achieved primarily through sets of contrasts, wherein 'the other' is marked as 'having race', whilst the normative white self is not marked as raced (as I suggested in the introductory chapter). This demonstrates what Fanon (1967) has termed 'epidermalisation', or as Hall (2000, p. 5) defines it: "the writing of difference on the skin of the other". Here difference becomes a function of the white self, which works to actively produce the location of the other-as-object (as opposed to actually representing the location of people who do not identify or who are not identified as white). From this perspective, I would suggest that epidermalisation thus marks the practice whereby difference is actually constructed on the terms of the same—racialised difference is structured upon the incorporation of incommensurable difference into a logic of sameness, whereby the location of those who refute white hegemony (e.g., Indigenous people in Australia) is incorporated into the self/other split produced under colonialism (Riggs, 2005a). Hook (2005) suggests much the same thing in his incisive analysis of the racial stereotype, where he expands and clarifies the work of Bhabha (1994). Hook, following Bhabha, suggests that the racial stereotype (particularly as it is enacted through the repetitive framing of particular presumed bodily forms of the racialised other) demonstrates an attempt to achieve the impossible: "the fixity of mutually exclusive subject categories for colonizer and colonized" (p. 13). This attempt at the impossible may be understood as a form of disavowal, as described earlier, aimed at erasing the anxiety that the existence of the racial other (as opposed to the racialised object of the stereotype) produces.

To clarify: my point here is that the co-option of difference (marked in this instance as race) into a logic of sameness (through, for example, the racial stereotype of the other) serves to deny the incommensurable differences that undermine white hegemony, and more specifically, white claims to ownership and belonging in Australia. My point in this section is thus not to further fetishise race, or to call for a 'return to the body', but instead to look at how the skin, which is conceptualised as the container of the body (and in particular those types of (white) bodies that accrue privilege within Australia), is both given such prominence in racialised accounts of subjectivity in Western nations, whilst at the same time the skin of white people is seldom ever mentioned (Winnubst, 2004). Discourses of race are thus not about 'describing' the differences between people, but about incorporating these differences into one particular way of understanding the world. Thus as Alcoff (1999, pp. 15-16) suggests, race as a practice of visibility works to "enclos[e] the entirety of difference within a taxonomy organized by a single logic". This point therefore demonstrates the importance of examining how race is materialised, and how it is used to legitimate practices of oppression.

In *Psychic Life of Power*, Butler (1997) provides a useful reading of Foucault's work on the prison. Whilst not talking about race, the following passage draws interesting and useful parallels with the materialisation of race:

> The materiality of the prison, Foucault writes, is established to the extent that (*dans la mesure ou*) it is a vector and instrument of power. Hence, the prison is *materialized* to the

extent that it is invested with power. To be grammatically accurate, there is no prison prior to its materialization; its materialization is coextensive with its investiture with power relations; and materiality is the effect and gauge of this investment. The prison comes to be only within the field of power relations, more specifically, only to the extent that it is saturated with such relation and that such a saturation is formative of its very being. Here the body–of the prisoner and the prison–is not an independent materiality, a static surface or site, which a subsequent investment comes to mark, signify upon, or pervade; the body is that for which materialization and investiture are coextensive. (p. 91; original emphasis)

Leaving aside the obvious connections between Foucault's work on the prison and the notion of 'race as a prison' (e.g., Muecke, 1992), I would suggest that this passage from Butler usefully extends my previous discussion of race as formative of subjectification. Indeed, it draws attention to the issue of accountability, and provides a more nuanced account of precisely how subjective investments work through the materialisation of race, and how this demonstrates the complicity of non-indigenous people in Australia with racism.

To elaborate: if, following Butler's (1997) logic, there is no 'race' prior to its materialisation, and if this materialisation occurs through the investment of race with power, then it would seem important to grasp how materialisation occurs concomitantly with subjectification. In other words, how does what I have previously said about the taking up of a collective memory of colonial violence become 'written' through the body–how is it that the materialisation of particular bodies as mattering occurs as a result of their location within ongoing histories of colonisation, and thus as products of practices of subjectification that occur within racialised networks of power? Towards the end of the passage Butler suggests a potential answer to this question, namely that "the body... is not an independent materiality... which a subsequent investment comes to mark... the body is that for which materialization and investiture are coextensive" (p. 91). In regards to race, then, the racialised body does not exist outside of a particular context, nor does the body become racialised upon the choosing of particular individuals. Rather, in the context of a nation built upon colonising desires (such as Australia), bodies come to matter precisely as markers of race that are used to shore up the colonising project. White bodies must thus be invested with race as a prerequisite for intelligibility within a nation that is founded upon racial difference as its source of legitimation. To do otherwise would be to deny the hegemony of white rule, or at the very least to acknowledge the legitimacy of Indigenous sovereignty. The question, then, is not whether the racialised body is brought into being through colonial power and is subsequently inhabited by a subject differentially invested in said power (or vice versa), but rather that white bodies are spoken into being specifically as colonial bodies–as bodies whose existence relies upon the corollary of particular subjective investments in the colonial project. In regards to subjectivity, then, the racialisation of bodies is the very grounds for subjectification– we come into being as knowers/subjects or objects in the form of particular racialised bodies.

It is important, however, to acknowledge here that this may at first seem to be a rather overdeterministic reading of racialised embodiment, and one that subsumes the experiences of Indigenous people (alongside others who are identified as 'non-white' within the Australian nation) yet again into a logic of 'difference in sameness', whereby racialisation occurs in the same ways (and for the same purpose) for all people. This is not my claim at all. Instead, my point has been to mark precisely how those bodies that are typically not designated as racialised (i.e., white bodies) come into being through discourses of race in relation to colonial power. This, as I see it, was a large part of Fanon's (1967) project–not to maintain a focus on how the white man constructs the black man, but how the white man constructs the white man *through* his constructions of the black man. Racism, and an investment in racialised practices (such as the materialisation of race), are thus formative of white subjectivities in Australia.

The important point that arises from this understanding of subject formation, then, is that the racialisation of white subjects is for the large part denied (in order to legitimate the *a priori* status of white privilege) by focusing on race as a 'regime of looking', whereby the white subject (rendered intelligible within networks of colonial power) does the looking, rather than being a recipient of a racialised gaze. Thus as Seshadri-Crooks (2000, p. 2) suggests, "although race cannot be reduced to the look... it is common knowledge that some 'black' people can be very white, and some 'whites' can be very dark; identity is a question of 'heritage', not skin colour. Once claimed, however, heritage is ultimately marked by the body... . Thus by visibility I refer to a regime of looking that thrives on 'major' and 'minor' details in order to shore up one's symbolic position". This 'regime of looking', as Seshadri-Crooks describes it, is one in which not only are white people the one's doing the looking, but it is subsequently the gaze of whiteness that produces bodily markers as being of significance.

This account of how race is materialised in conjunction with racial subjectification demonstrates precisely how it is that white queer people stand to benefit from racialised hierarchies. If particular queer people are identified as white as a product of particular visual markers, then regardless of other 'markers' that may be seen to designate queerness, the markers of whiteness will continue to accrue privilege to white queers. To 'be' a white queer in this sense is not to inhabit a particular identity *per se,* but rather to be located within a relationship to particular normative assumptions surrounding racial markers and racial difference. As I will discuss in the following section, these points hold important implications for how we understand 'queer identities', and how we conceptualise the category of 'the individual'.

Queer Identities/Social Practices

One of the implications of the previous elaboration of how white people are always already racialised in relation to particular histories of white violence is that it provides an account of 'identity' that is not reliant upon an individualised or internalised account of what it means to be a subject. In other words, by seeing race as produced through a set of social hierarchies that institute difference on the terms of the same, and by seeing subjectivities as shaped by the intelligible forms of racial being that are sanctioned by the state, it is possible to see identities not as things possessed by individuals, but rather that 'individual identities' are themselves social practices. To be recognised as a white person who claims particular forms of privilege in a racist society is not to do so as an individual person who stands up and decides 'I want some privilege'. Rather, to be recognised as an intelligible white subject is to already be seen as entitled to privilege (however differentially that may be distributed). Such recognition occurs not because an 'individual' demands it, but rather because it is the recognition of another as a sovereign being that is constitutive of the act of being in the first place. To be recognised as a white queer is thus to have one's location within racialised hierarchies affirmed.

This argument about identities may be made clearer if we turn to look at what it means to claim an identity that does not share the same luxury of recognition that is afforded by white privilege. To speak as a non-white queer person may well be to speak and not to be heard *on one's own terms*. To be told, as a queer Indigenous person, for example, that your claims to land title will not be recognised, or that your rights to enter a hospital in the first place in order to see your sick partner can be denied on the basis of race (as I suggested in Chapter Four), is to be told that the social practices through which your identity is constituted are not valid. To have your identity recognised as a *white* queer person (or as a white straight person for that matter) is to have your identity recognised as a particular type of person—as one who accepts the terms for recognition set by the state, or whose identity most closely mirrors that of the normative white subject.

Understanding identities as social practices rather than as individual possessions thus holds the potential for understanding how it is that white queers are so easily assimilated into the imaginary of the white nation: as white people, white queers are largely already recognised as nominal members of a dominant group. Our privilege is already in place, and our location within a relationship to privilege always already props up the social practices of whiteness that render us intelligible in the first place. As such, white (queer) identities are neither solely social nor individual in nature—they are in and of themselves social artefacts that are simultaneously produced through social contexts, whilst being productive of social contexts, in that their ongoing reiteration serves to further enshrine the normative status of whiteness.

These points about identities as social practices beg the question of where to go next when attempting to frame queer rights on the part of white queers. One potential response is provided by Judith Butler (in Bell, 1999), who suggests that "the real task is to figure out how a subject who is constituted in and by discourse then recites that very same discourse but perhaps to another purpose. For me that's always been the question of how to find agency, the moment of that recitation or that replay of discourse that is the condition of one's own emergence" (p. 165).

How can it be possible, then, for white queers to engage in a discourse of identity in regards to rights that recites that discourse, but for purposes that were perhaps not its original intention? If rights in liberal democracies are generally seen as a means to securing the greatest good for the greatest number, then how can it be possible for white queers to recite this type of mantra without it resulting in yet more blanket moral statements about what constitutes 'good' (as I suggested in Chapter Four), or in more claims to 'love' that actually exclude particular queers from ever claiming a position of love (as I suggested in Chapter Five)? And more specifically, how can the very discourse of rights, which is largely configured through individual identity claims, be spoken in ways that actually reconfigure the modes of identity that currently circulate in colonial nations—how may rights discourse produce a focus on social accountability that, I have proposed, must be a precursor to the securing of rights for white queer people? These are questions that I turn to in the final section of this chapter.

State Moral Minimalism

Throughout this chapter I have placed considerable emphasis on examining how it is that white queers are invested in a logic of possession that is configured through histories of white violence in Australia. Moreover, I have sought to challenge the assumption that such a logic is the product of *individual* investments, and instead have shown how such investments are foundationally social practices that produce a semblance of individuality and thus reproduce white hegemony. Far from being a deterministic account of racialisation and identity, as it may appear at first glance, it instead opens up an account of subjectification that demonstrates the radical potential for reconfiguring how white queers relate to state sanction. This would not be so to claim a space outside of whiteness, nor to disclaim accountability for unearned race privilege. Instead, it is about looking at how white queers who seek rights on the terms set by the state may ultimately serve to perpetuate the normative status of rights under white hegemony.

In contrast to much queer rights rhetoric, which often accepts the framework of liberal individualism as its starting place, we may instead focus our attention on reconfiguring how rights advocacy may constitute a critique of the very notion of state sanction itself. In his work on marriage and civil rights, Halle (2001) proposes that the work of the Cambridge Lavender Alliance[1] (CLA) may be instructive for understanding how rights claims may be reconfigured so as to be less reliant upon the state as the primary locus of sanction. Halle suggests that the concept of 'state moral minimalism' may be a useful means for both exposing the biases that are inherent to the law, and for negotiating forms of state-based support that do not require the current high level of state control over the lives of queer people. Thus he reports that the CLA resolution on same-sex marriage "made no mention of marriage at all; rather, it... required of the state that it withdraw from the regulation of marriage, thereby allowing for a de facto expansion of the parameters of civil society" (p. 388). Such an approach draws attention to the moral judgments that inhere to the law, whilst also suggesting that morality should not be something that is arbitrated by the state.

Such an approach to activism may assist queer people in refusing the terms set by the state for debates over queer rights. Likewise, to some degree the notion of state moral minimalism may sidestep the problems that arise from further promoting a particular form of relationality (such as marriage) that will potentially exclude many people and relationships. To return to the APA resolution on same-sex marriage discussed in Chapter Three, I would propose that such a resolution need not take a position that involves accepting the terms for recognition set by the state. Instead, the APA (for example) could develop resolutions that start by highlighting the role that both the discipline of psychology and the state have played in oppressing queer people. This would allow not only for some reflection on why law reform is needed (i.e., not

---

[1] The Cambridge Lavender Alliance (CLA) is the key queer political organisation in Cambridge, Massachusetts. It has a long history of queer activism, and has recently endorsed candidates for election within the US. The CLA has often been particularly forward thinking in its approach to queer politics, as was highlighted in its early position on the push for marriage rights.

for queer people to gain 'equality with' heterosexual people, but because the law is founded upon heterosexist norms that are discriminatory), but would also provide a space within which multiple simultaneous forms of oppression could be examined in the context of the lives of queer people. Such a resolution could, for example, highlight how notions of miscegenation have historically informed marriage laws, and the implications of this for how the law is racialised (Moreton-Robinson, 2004a). By starting from a focus on how social norms are produced, and how they exclude or oppress certain groups of people, it may be possible to develop a position on queer rights that need not reinforce liberal notions of 'equality with'. Likewise, a focus on the multiple effects of the law upon the lives of those who experience oppression may enable white middle-class queers (amongst others) to explore not only how we experience oppression, but how we at the same time stand to benefit from racialised norms. A resolution framed in this way may focus on how rights are often founded upon the exclusion of certain groups, an approach that would encourage critical examination of how complicity or domestication operate. By understanding rights in a relational (rather than individual) way, it may be easier to conceptualise how privilege is made possible through oppression, and how rights claims are framed by our belonging to particular marginalised or dominant groups.

Finally, a focus on state moral minimalism may be useful for challenging not only how we see the rights of queer people, but how we understand the rights of all people living in colonial nations: state mandated rights are imposed not only upon queer people, but upon all citizens. Rather than focusing on how we can engage with the state in order to gain sanction, we may instead focus on the limitations of state sanction (as it is currently configured) for all people (Butler, 2002). This may help to challenge the stranglehold that liberal politics hold over current understandings of rights. This call for an engagement with notions of state sanction thus challenges white queer rights advocates to examine how we conceptualise the role of the state, as well as the model of subjectivity that it presumes. In other words, it is important to examine what the potential outcomes may be from simply amending laws to include queer (white) people *as individual people*, whilst leaving the racism and heterosexism of the law unchallenged. What is required, then, is not a disengagement from social advocacy *per se*, but rather a more explicit examination of particular moral investments in 'good society', and how such investments are complicit with the legitimation of oppressive practices. Likewise, it is important that any approach to social advocacy acknowledges the specificity of its claims. Otherwise, there is always the risk that the promotion of one particular form of rights (e.g., for lesbians and gay men) may effectively silence or marginalise the rights of another group (such as bisexual or transgendered individuals). This suggests that rather than continuing to solely engage in single issue politics that do not explicitly talk about their attendant moral assumptions, we need to engage in a socially accountable practice that explores histories of oppression and is thus mindful of how these histories continue to shape the ways we engage in advocacy and rights today (Riggs, 2004e).

These points in regards to state sanction and accountability may go some way towards addressing Butler's (1999) points in regards to agency. If the rights claims of white queers are in some respect constitutive of particular white queer identity claims (as I have elaborated through this book), then how may alternate understandings of rights (such as state moral minimalism, for example) constitute a recitation of rights discourse that actually reconfigures its purpose? My suggestion is thus not that white queers need to stop making rights claims, or that white queer people can escape race privilege, but rather that the very ways in which we claim rights can contribute to a reshaping of how both queer rights and queer identities are understood. If rights claims are made not to secure sanction for individual white queers *per se*, but rather to challenge the very process of state sanction itself, then white queers may contribute, if not to the downfall of white heteropatriarchy, then at the very least to a destabilisation of how white privilege operates, and thus begin a move towards collaborative partnerships with queers who do not identify as white that are based upon a recognition of ongoing histories of white violence, and which take the need for accountability as their starting place.

Chapter Summary

In this final chapter I have provided an alternate account of how we may understand identities as social practices, and I have demonstrated the utility of this for examining how white queers are invested in the possessive logic of patriarchal white sovereignty as a result of our racialised subject positions. Through an extended discussion of one particular understanding of how white racial subjectification operates, I have highlighted what it means to claim rights as a white queer person, and have demonstrated the need to reconceptualise rights in ways that (a) centre on accountability and an ethical engagement with Indigenous sovereignty as the ground upon which we walk, (b) refuse to reify state sanction as it is currently configured, and (c) take as their starting place an understanding of subjectivity that questions the individualistic logic that would appear to permeate human rights claims.

My intention throughout this book has been neither to simply attack existing rights claims and then posit a 'solution', nor to claim the moral high ground in relation to white queer rights and race privilege. Instead, my aim has been to outline an engagement with the problematic that I raised at the beginning of the introductory chapter, namely, how can 'we' research differing forms of oppression and privilege simultaneously, and who is referred to when the third person plural is used. My engagement with this problematic has taken a number of forms, including (a) an elaboration of why it is that researching simultaneous 'identities' seems at first to be difficult, (b) an examination of how particular identity claims privilege particular white queer accounts of subjectivity, (c) an interrogation of what it means to identify as white in a colonial nation such as Australia, and (d) an engagement with Indigenous critiques of white privilege. By exploring these intersecting forms of engagement, I have elaborated an understanding of queer *in conjunction with privilege* that unsettles the presumed-to-be difficulty of doing just that.

My interest in identities, and in particular their relation to rights, has thus produced an account of queer rights that turns neither on issues of identities or rights, but rather speaks of what it means to be accountable for one's own location and privilege in a postcolonial nation. In producing a situated account of white queer privilege *as a white gay man,* I have repeatedly returned to this focus—why accountability is of such vital importance, and how it can be engaged without resorting to moralising accounts of right or wrong. Thus, as Fiona Nicoll (2004a) suggests, instead of seeking to 'solve racism' or 'give up power' by being 'better' white people, it is important that those of us who identify as white queers recognise that the belief in the 'goodness' of white people is precisely the foundation of practices of oppression in Australia. What I have called for here instead is not a 'black armband' account of colonisation, as Prime Minister Howard would have us believe, but rather a calling to account of how white privilege operates, and how it appears in places that to some (white queer) people may seem surprising, whilst to others may seem entirely commonplace and expected. To confront the multifarious nature of white hegemony in Australia is thus to be willing (for those of us who identify as white) to be rendered uncomfortable in the face of complicity, and to engage, rather than refute, our own locations.

In conclusion, I return to my initial examination in Chapter One of the film *The Adventures of Priscilla, Queen of the Desert*, and I examine how it provides us with at least two examples of how white queer belonging in Australia is unsettled often at the very moment where it is claimed. In the first example from the film, we see the bus stop abruptly when the driver (one of the white queer characters) first sees the massive expanse of the desert. The three white queer characters step down from the bus to take in the enormity of what they face, and in that moment, when one of them suggests 'maybe we should have flown', we hear the music of didgeridoos, an instrument most commonly associated within Indigenous people. This I take as an example of the awe and potential fear that the white queer characters are faced with when they are forced to engage with something they either cannot comprehend, or which cannot be easily assimilated. As a result, whilst the white queer characters are engaged in traversing a landscape to which they claim belonging, the landscape itself challenges this claim to belonging. Furthermore, the didgeridoos that we hear would seem to suggest that whilst the landscape would appear to be somehow 'uncanny' or unfamiliar to the white queers, it may not be so to Indigenous people (at least those who play didgeridoos!). Whilst of course it is problematic that the landscape is automatically associated with didgeridoo music, it nonetheless serves to demonstrate the anxiety that white Australians often hold in regards to belonging in this country.

The second example of how white queer belonging is unsettled appears in what may be read as the penultimate moment of the movie. One of the characters (the one who had previously abruptly halted the bus ride) tells earlier in the movie of the fact that 'ever since I was a lad I've had this dream, a dream that I now, finally, have a chance to fulfill: to travel to the centre of Australia, climb Kings Canyon (as a queen), in a full-length-Gaultier-sequinned, heels and a tiara'. Following their arrival in Alice Springs, and the subsequent storyline there, the three white queer characters proceed to do just that: climb a rather large mountain in full drag. Yet when they stand at the top, seemingly queens of all they survey, there appears to be a gap between the desire for the type of belonging or unity that the dream may have suggested, and the actuality of it. Once they are all 'at the top', Bernadette states 'It never ends. All that space'. To which the 'lad with the dream' asks 'so what now?' The third character responds by saying 'I think I wanna go home'. This to me signifies the characters' recognition of a disjuncture between the dream of being in the imagined space 'at the top of Kings Canyon', and the desire to 'be at home': belonging does not appear to come easily being dressed in drag at the 'centre of Australia'. This is not of course to say that white queers are *a priori* excluded from belonging 'at the centre', but rather that dreams of belonging, which I would suggest inform a significant part of a white national imaginary, are not so easily fulfilled when faced with 'all that space'. Home is something that the white queer characters 'go back to', rather than being something they carry with them, in contrast to what Aileen Moreton-Robinson (2003) has referred to as Indigenous people's 'ontological relationship to land'–that Indigenous people carry their sovereign rights to belonging with them through their embodiment. White queer belonging in *Priscilla* is thus depicted as predicated on an anxious form of embodied belonging that only exists in particular 'settled locations' that are taken as signifying in excess of 'all that space'.

So, to summarise, and to return to the paper by Padva (2002) one last time: camp, as represented in films such as *Priscilla*, is not inherently political, where the term 'political' suggests subversive or critical. Yes, certainly, *Priscilla* has a politics about it, one that speaks out about homophobia, stereotypes and queer identity. But that does not necessarily make it politically useful in the context of a postcolonising nation. Thus in contrast to Padva, who suggests that Susan Sontag's seminal text on camp misreads camp's political intent, I would *not* concur with his statement that "[camp] subculture's subversive aspects in fact politically challenge the social and cultural order" (p. 217). Whilst it may be true that camp challenges particular aspects of the social order, as do queer politics and theory, they largely do so from the perspective of white queers, and with the agendas set by white queers. Camp, just like queer, may at times do much more than that, but to assume that they automatically do so would be to miss something crucial: that critiques of oppression may not themselves be free from enacting oppression. As I have suggested throughout this book, it is thus important that those of us who identify as proponents of white queer politics in a postcolonising nation such as Australia examine our own assumptions, and challenge the privileges that we may presume.

☙ Postscript

As I write today following the election here in South Australia, I am reminded of the continued need for those of us who identify as white queers to interrogate the simultaneous occurrences of sexualised oppression and race privilege that shape our lives. Prior to the election, the local queer rights lobby (represented by the *Let's Get Equal* campaign, as discussed in Chapter Four) circulated a document outlining the commitment of each major party to queer rights legislation. The Labor party was ranked third in its commitment to queer rights (behind Democrats first and Greens second). In this sense it has been heartening to see such a strong swing within the election towards both the Greens and the Labor party, and one can only hope that these parties will continue to support a queer rights agenda.

Sadly, however, there was also a swing towards the Family First party, ranked at the bottom of the list in the aforementioned document. Indeed, in my own electorate the Family First party captured a little over 4% of the vote, coming just behind the Democrats. Whilst 4% may seem like a small number, it is nonetheless important to keep in mind that there was approximately a 3 point swing *towards* the Family First party across the entire state of South Australia. Much like the phenomenon of the One Nation party that rose to relative power back in the late 1990s, the Family First party is one that is not going to simply go away by ignoring it. Campaigns that raise awareness and challenge discrimination, and research that seeks to examine what it is that motivates the types of sentiment that informs parties such as Family First, are of vital importance within the broader picture of research on queer experience.

Of note also was the fact that the One Nation party still managed to secure 0.8% of the vote for South Australia, despite its relative lack of visibility post the heady days of Hansonism in the late 1990s. Whilst this may seem like a very small percentage of the vote, it may be compared with the percentage of votes received by an independent member running under the banner 'Aboriginal Representation and Reconciliation', who received only 0.1% of the vote. When I was in the polling booth, the juxtaposition of these two parties on the voting slips triggered memories of my own concerns about the Family First party, as I elaborated in Chapter Six. My automatic reaction when ranking candidates for the upper house was to put Family First right at the bottom. Yet at the same time it seemed questionable to place One Nation higher than Family First–whose politics should I privilege–my own queer politics (which are being undermined by the Family First party, but which in principle supports reconciliation), or a politics of racial justice, for which One Nation would rank at the very bottom? Of course it is no doubt of little relevance whether I ranked one at the bottom and the other just above that. My point is not about the power of my vote *per se*, but rather about the allegiances that we choose in our everyday lives, and the terms on which we fight our battles.

What made this dilemma all the more salient was that prior to the election I could not wait for the Family First placards bearing the slogan 'Protect your family' to come down. As I drove past them every day, often on the way to dropping off or picking up the child I care for, it offended me to see such slogans, telling me that I am one of the 'elements' from which the families referred to in the placards (i.e., heterosexual nuclear families) require protection. Of course on the one hand there may be some utility in examining why it is that parties such as Family First consider themselves to be 'on the run' from, or 'threatened' by, the challenge that queer families may present to the heterosexual nuclear family. Nonetheless, it was offensive to see placards on a daily basis that implicitly tell me (and other queer people) that we are a threat to someone else's safety.

My response to these placards was of course not a desire to be 'included' within the rhetoric of the family promoted by Family First. Nor however was it to claim some point of 'essential difference' outside of the category of 'family' (Riggs, forthcoming). Rather, the question for me was about what it means to be positioned as a threat, and how such a positioning for white queers is relative to the positioning of other groups of people (such as refugees, Indigenous people, and those homogeneously referred to as being of 'Asian descent') as inherently threatening to the white Australian nation. As I suggested in Chapter Five, whilst on the one hand white queers are often denied a space within everyday understandings of families and parenting, we nonetheless stand to benefit from the ongoing ways in which non-white people (queer or otherwise) are denied a place within the nation.

It thus continues to be important to question what it means to be a white lesbian (for example) walking down the street with a child, not having to worry about having her hijab ripped off in the current context of anti-Muslim sentiment, or to be a white gay man spending a day out shopping with other white friends, at little risk of being accused of shoplifting or loitering on the basis of his race, or to speak out as a white bisexual woman, with little likelihood of being told 'all of your race are troublemakers'. And it is likewise important to examine these experiences, and compare them to those of Muslim women constantly at threat of racist violence, or Indigenous people who are often under suspicion for non-existent crimes (or who are often not adequately assisted when they themselves are victims of crimes), or Lebanese people who, in the context of the recent white riots in Cronulla, were depicted as a 'dangerous race'. These wide-ranging experiences are not unrelated, and it is only the race privilege of white queers that allows us to believe otherwise. Privilege is always the flip-side of discrimination and oppression, and whilst it seems that for the foreseeable future queer people in general will continue to have to push for some form of rights, it does not have to be the case that these rights are seen as separable from a cultural context within which white queers continue to benefit from a social order that prioritises white values and ways of being in the world.

Damien W. Riggs
Adelaide
April 2006

❧ References

Ahmed, S. (2003). In the name of love. *Borderlands e-journal, 2*. Retrieved August 14, 2005, from http://www.borderlandsejournal.adelaide.edu.au

Ahmed, S. (2004). *The cultural politics of emotion*. Edinburgh: Edinburgh University Press.

Aldrich, R. (2003). *Colonialism and homosexuality*. London: Routledge.

American Psychological Association. (2004). *Resolution on sexual orientation and marriage*. Retrieved January 10, 2005, from http://www.apa.org/pi/lgbc/policy/marriage.pdf

Australian Marriage Equality. (2005). *The case for equal marriage*. Retrieved 1 May, 2006, from http://www.australianmarriageequality.com

Barker, M. (2004). This is my partner, and this is my... partner's partner: Constructing a polyamorous identity in a monogamous world. *International Journal of Constructivist Psychology, 18*, 75-88.

Barnard, I. (2003). *Queer race: Interventions in the racial politics of queer theory*. New York: Peter Lang.

Bell, V. (1999). On speech, race and melancholia: An interview with Judith Butler. *Theory, Culture and Society, 16*, 163-174.

Bernstein, M. (2001). Gender, queer family policies, and the limits of the law. In M. Bernstein & R. Reimann (Eds.), *Queer families, queer politics: Challenging culture and the state* (pp. 420-446). New York: Columbia University Press.

Bĕrubĕ, A. (2001). How gay stays white and what kind of white it stays. In B.B. Rasmussen, E. Klinenberg, I.J. Nexica & M. Wray (Eds.), *The making and unmaking of whiteness* (pp. 234-265). Durham: Duke University Press.

Brown, W. (1994). *States of injury*. Princeton, NJ: Princeton University Press.

Butler, J. (1997). *Psychic life of power*. Stanford: Stanford University Press.

Butler, J. (2002). Is kinship always already heterosexual? *Differences: A Feminist Journal of Cultural Studies, 13*, 14-44.

Butler, J. (2004). *Precarious life*. New York: Verso.

Chesterman, S. (1998). Human rights as subjectivity: The age of rights and the politics of culture. *Millennium: Journal of International Studies, 27*, 97-117.

Clarke, V. (2000) Lesbian mothers: Sameness and difference. *Feminism & Psychology, 10*, 273-278.

Clarke, V. (2002). Sameness and difference in research on lesbian parenting. *Journal of Community & Applied Social Psychology, 12*, 210-222.

Clarke, V., & Kitzinger, C. (2004). Lesbian and gay parents on talk shows: Resistance or collusion in heterosexism? *Qualitative Research in Psychology, 1*, 195-217.

Coalition for Equality. (2005). *New national human rights voice for gays.* Retrieved 1 May, 2006, from http://www.coalitionforequality.org.au

Connors, L. (1994). Two opposed traditions: Male popular culture and the criminal justice system in early Queensland. In R. Aldrich (Ed.), *Gay perspectives 2: More essays in Australian gay culture* (pp. 83-114). Sydney: University of Sydney Press.

Coombs, M. (2001). Transgenderism and sexual orientation: More than a marriage of convenience? In M. Bernstein & R. Reimann (Eds.), *Queer families, queer politics: Challenging culture and the state* (pp. 397-419). New York: Columbia University Press.

Crossley, M. (2000). *Rethinking health psychology.* Hampshire: Open University Press.

Crossley, M. (2004). Making sense of 'barebacking': Gay men's narratives, unsafe sex and the 'resistance habitus'. *British Journal of Social Psychology, 43*, 225-244.

Egale. (2003). *Registered partnerships are offensive and unworkable segregation.* Retrieved May 8, 2006, from http://www.egale.ca

Ettelbrick, P.L. (1989). Since when is marriage a path to liberation? *Out/Look: National Gay and Lesbian Quarterly, 9*, 14-16.

Fine, M. (1997). Witnessing Whiteness. In M. Fine, L. Weis, L.C. Powell & L. Mun Wong (Eds.), *Off white: Readings on race, power and society* (pp. 111-122). New York: Routledge.

Finn, T. (2002). *Submission to Connecticut legislative hearing on same-sex marriage.* Retrieved 10 August, 2005, from http://www.cga.ct.gov/jud/SameSexMarriage/Finn_testimony.pdf

Fogarty, W.J. (1992). 'Certain habits': The development of the concept of the male homosexual in New South Wales law, 1788-1900. In R. Aldrich & G. Wotherspoon (Eds.), *Gay perspectives: Essays in Australian gay culture* (pp. 59-76). Sydney: University of Sydney Press.

Frye, M. (1990). A response to *Lesbian Ethics. Hypatia, 5*, 132-137.

Gays and Lesbians Aboriginal Alliance. (1994). Peopling the empty mirror: The prospects for lesbian and gay Aboriginal history. In R. Aldrich (Ed.), *Gay perspectives 2: More essays in Australian gay culture* (pp. 1-62). Sydney: University of Sydney Press.

Grant, B. (1997). *Pauline Hanson: One Nation and Australian politics*. Armidale: University of New England Press.

Hage, G. (1998). *White nation: Fantasies of white supremacy in a multicultural society*. Annandale: Pluto Press.

Hage, G. (2003). *Against paranoid nationalism: Searching for hope in a shrinking society*. Annandale: Pluto Press.

Haggis, J. (2005). Beyond race and whiteness? Reflections on the new abolitionists and an Australian critical whiteness studies. In D.W. Riggs (Ed.), *Taking up the challenge: Critical race and whiteness studies in a postcolonising nation*. Adelaide: Crawford House Publishers.

Halle, R. (2001). Political organizing and the limits of civil rights: Gay marriage and queer families. In M. Bernstein & R. Reimann (Eds.), *Queer families, queer politics: Challenging culture and the state* (pp. 379-398). New York: Columbia University Press.

Hanson, P. (1996). Maiden speech. *Hansard*, House of Representatives. September 10, 3860-3863.

Harding, R. (2005). Psychology, human rights and law: The case of planned lesbian families. *Lesbian and Gay Psychology Review, 6*, 23-34.

Harris, A.P. (1995). Race and essentialism in feminist legal theory. In R. Delago (Ed.), *Critical race theory: The cutting edge* (pp. 75-82). Philadelphia: Temple University Press.

Hegarty, P., & Chase, C. (2005). Intersex activism, feminism and psychology. In I. Morland & A. Willox (Eds.), *Queer theory* (pp. 158-170). Hampshire: Palgrave.

Hill, L. (1998). Pauline Hanson, free speech and reconciliation. *Journal of Australian Studies, 57*, 10-22.

Hook, D. (2005). Paradoxes of the other: (Post)colonial racism, racial difference, stereotype-as-fetish. *Psychology in Society, 31*, 9-30.

hooks, b. (1981). *Ain't I a woman: Black women and feminism*. Boston: South End Press.

hooks, b. (1989). *Talking back: Thinking feminist, thinking black*. Boston: South End Press.

hooks, b. (1992). Representing whiteness in the black imagination. In L. Grossberg, C. Nelson & P. Treichler (Eds.), *Cultural studies* (pp. 338-46). New York: Routledge.

Irigaray, L. (2002). *The way of love*. London: Continuum.

Johnson, C. (2002). Heteronormative citizenship and the politics of passing. *Sexualities, 5,* 317-336.

Johnson, C. (2003). Heteronormative citizenship: The Howard government's views on gay and lesbian issues. *Australian Journal of Political Science, 38,* 45-62.

Johnson-Riordan, L. (2005). Loving differently, becoming other-wise. Cultural studies/whiteness studies and (public) pedagogies for reconciliation. In D.W. Riggs (Ed.), *Taking up the challenge: Critical race and whiteness studies in a postcolonising nation.* Adelaide: Crawford Publishers.

Kitzinger, C., & Perkins, R. (1993). *Changing our minds: Lesbian feminism and psychology.* New York: New York University Press.

Kitzinger, C., & Wilkinson, S. (2004a). The re-branding of marriage: Why we got married rather than registering a civil partnership. *Feminism & Psychology, 14,* 127-150.

Kitzinger, C., & Wilkinson, S. (2004b). Social advocacy for equal marriage: The politics of 'rights' and the psychology of 'mental health'. *Analyses of Social Issues and Public Policy,* 4. Retrieved May 25, 2006, from http://www.asap-spssi.org/default.htm

Lane, C. (1995). *The ruling passion: British colonial allegory and the paradox of homosexual desire.* Durham: Duke University Press.

Langdridge, D. (2005). Editorial: Three responses to *Making sense of barebacking. Lesbian and Gay Psychology Review, 6,* 43-44.

Leach, M., Stokes, G., & Ward, I. (2000). *The rise and fall of One Nation.* St. Lucia: University of Queensland Press.

Loader, M. (2004). A recipe for recognition of same sex relationships. Accessed May 15, 2005, from http://www.letsgetequal.org.au/FeministLegalAcademics.doc

Lipsitz, G. (1998). *The possessive investment in whiteness: How white people profit from identity politics.* Philadelphia: Temple University Press.

Mama, A. (1995). *Beyond the masks: Race, gender and subjectivity.* London: Routledge.

McKinnon, C. (2005). *Women's lives, men's laws.* Massachusetts: Belknap Press.

Moreton-Robinson, A. (2000). *Talkin' up to the white women: Indigenous women and feminism.* St. Lucia: University of Queensland Press.

Moreton-Robinson, A. (2003). I still call Australia home: Indigenous belonging and place in a white postcolonizing society. In S. Ahmed, C. Castañeda, A. Fortier & M. Sheller (Eds.), *Uprootings/regroundings: Questions of home and migration* (pp. 131-149). Oxford: Berg.

Moreton-Robinson, A. (2004a). The possessive logic of patriarchal white sovereignty: The high court and the Yorta Yorta decision. *Borderlands e-journal 3(2)*. Retrieved May 25, 2005, from http://www.borderlandsejournal.adelaide.edu.au

Moreton-Robinson, A. (2004b). Indigenous sovereignty and the politics of race: A possessive investment in patriarchal white sovereignty. Keynote presented at the *Body Politic conference*, Brisbane, Queensland, 24-26 November.

Nicolacopoulos, T., & Vassilacopoulos, G. (2004). Racism, foreigner communities and the onto-pathology of white Australian subjectivity. In A. Moreton-Robinson (Ed.), *Whitening race: Essays in social and cultural criticism* (pp. 32-47). Canberra: Aboriginal Studies Press.

Nicoll, F. (2000). Indigenous sovereignty and the violence of perspective: A white woman's coming out story. *Australian Feminist Studies, 15*, 369-386.

Nicoll, F. (2001). *From diggers to drag queens: Configurations of Australian national identity*. Annandale: Pluto Press.

Nicoll, F. (2004a). 'Are you calling me a racist?' Teaching critical whiteness theory in Indigenous sovereignty. *Borderlands e-journal, 3*. Retrieved August 9, 2005, from http://www.borderlandsejournal.adelaide.edu.au

Nicoll, F. (2004b). After Keating: Queer(y)ing ordinary mums and dads. In D. Carter (Ed.), *The ideas market* (pp. 145-163). Melbourne: Melbourne University Press.

Nuremberg Law. (1935). *Law for the protection of German blood and German honour*. Retrieved 8 June, 2006, from http://www.jewishvirtuallibrary.org

O'Doherty, K., & Augoustinos, M. (2005). Australia and the Tampa: The use of nationalist rhetoric to legitimate military action and the marginalisation of asylum seekers. In D.W. Riggs (Ed.), *Taking up the challenge: Critical race and whiteness studies in a post-colonising nation*. Adelaide: Crawford Publishers.

Offord, B. (2003). *Homosexual rights as human rights*. New York: Peter Lang.

Padva, G. (2000). Priscilla fights back: The politicization of camp subculture. *Journal of Communication Inquiry, 24*, 216-243.

Phelan, S. (2001). *Sexual strangers: Gays, lesbians, and dilemmas of citizenship*. Philadelphia: Temple University Press.

Pollack, S., & Vaughn, J. (1987). *Politics of the heart: A lesbian parenting anthology*. New York: Firebrand Books.

Povinelli, E. (2002). Notes on gridlock: Genealogy, intimacy, sexuality. *Public Culture, 14*, 215-238.

Rapley, M. (1998). 'Just an ordinary Australian': Self-categorization and the discursive construction of facticity in 'new racist' political rhetoric. *British Journal of Social Psychology, 37,* 325-344.

Rich, A. (1996). *Blood, bread and poetry.* New York: W. W. Norton.

Richards, G. (1997). *'Race', racism and psychology: Towards a reflexive history.* New York: Routledge.

Riggs, D.W. (2004a). Resisting heterosexism in foster carer training: Valuing queer approaches to adult learning and relationality. *Canadian Journal of Queer Studies in Education, 1.* Retrieved June 16, 2005, from http://jqstudies.oise. utoronto.ca/journal

Riggs, D.W. (2004b). The politics of scientific knowledge: Constructions of sexuality and ethics in the conversion therapy literature. *Lesbian & Gay Psychology Review, 5,* 6-14.

Riggs, D.W. (2004c). Constructing the national good: Howard and the rhetoric of benevolence. In *Conference Proceedings of the Australasian Political Studies Association Conference.* The University of Adelaide. Retrieved May 20, 2005, from http://www. adelaide.edu.au/apsa/docs_papers/Others/Riggs.pdf

Riggs, D.W. (2004d). Benevolence and the management of stake: On being 'good white people'. *Philament: A Journal of the Arts and Culture, 4.* Retrieved August 14, 2005, from http://www.arts.usyd. edu.au/publications/philament

Riggs, D.W. (2004e). Challenging the monoculturalism of psychology: Towards a more socially accountable pedagogy and practice. *Australian Psychologist, 39,* 110-126.

Riggs, D.W. (2005a). Caught 'n 'e frame?: The gender illusionist within heteropatriarchy. *Philament: An Online Journal of the Arts and Culture, 7.* Retrieved March 5, 2006, from http://www.arts.usyd. edu.au/publications/philament

Riggs, D.W. (2005b). 'Proving the case': Psychology, subjectivity and representations of lesbian and gay parents in the media. In L. Castañeda & S. Campbell (Eds.), *News and Sexuality: Media Portraits of Diversity* (pp. 235-255). New York: Sage.

Riggs, D.W. (2006a). Psychology, queer rights, and unearned moral authority. *Asylum, 15.*

Riggs, D.W. (2006b). What's love got to do with it? Ambivalence and the national imaginary. *International Journal of Critical Psychology, 16,* 32-52.

Riggs, D.W. (2006c). Developmentalism and the rhetoric of 'best interests of the child': Challenging heteronormative constructions of families and parenting in foster care. *Journal of GLBT Family Studies, 2,* 57-73.

Riggs, D.W. (forthcoming). *Becoming parent: Lesbians, gay men, and family*. Perth: Brightfire Press.

Riggs, D.W., & Augoustinos, M. (2004). Projecting threat: Managing subjective investments in whiteness. *Psychoanalysis, Culture & Society, 9*, 219-236.

Riggs, D.W., & Augoustinos, M. (2005). The psychic life of colonial power: Racialised subjectivities, bodies, and methods. *Journal of Community and Applied Social Psychology, 15*, 461-477.

Riggs, D.W., & Choi, P.Y.L. (2006). Heterosexism, racism and psychology: Challenging or colluding with privilege? *The Psychologist, 19*, 288-291.

Riggs, D.W., & Riggs, L.D. (2004). Talking about heterosexism: Politics, complicity and identification. In D.W. Riggs & G.A. Walker (Eds.), *Out in the antipodes: Australian and New Zealand perspectives on gay and lesbian issues in psychology* (pp. 416-434). Perth: Brightfire Press.

Riggs, D.W., & Walker, G.A. (2004). Quite contrary: Lesbian and gay psychology in the antipodes. In D.W. Riggs & G.A. Walker (Eds.), *Out in the antipodes: Australian and New Zealand perspectives on gay and lesbian issues in psychology* (pp. 1-23). Perth: Brightfire Press.

Riggs, D.W., & Walker, G.A. (2006). Queer(y)ing rights: Psychology, liberal individualism and colonisation. *Australian Psychologist, 41*, 95-103.

Robson, R. (1992). Mother: The legal domestication of lesbian existence. *Hypatia, 7*, 172-185.

Rofes, E. (1998). Innocence, perversion, and *Heather's Two Mommies*. *Journal of Gay, Lesbian, and Bisexual Identity, 3*, 3-26.

Rogers, G., & Booth, A. (2004). Queer goings-on: A genealogy of lesbian and gay psychology. In D.W. Riggs & G.A. Walker (Eds.), *Out in the antipodes: Australian and New Zealand perspectives on gay and lesbian issues in psychology* (pp. 25-55). Perth: Brightfire Press.

Rutherford, J. (2002). *The gauche intruder*. Melbourne: Melbourne University Press.

Smith, B., & Diehl, K. (2000). Here's the movement, let's start the building. *Colorlines, 3*. Accessed June 7, 2006, from http://www.arc.org/C_Lines/CLArchive/story3_3_05.html

Smith, L.T. (1999). *Decolonizing methodologies*. London: Zed Books.

Spurlin, W.J. (2005). I'd rather be the princess than the queen! Mourning Diana as a gay icon. In I. Morland & A. Willox (Eds.), *Queer theory* (pp. 158-167). Hampshire: Palgrave.

Steinberg, D.L. (1997). Technologies of heterosexuality: Eugenic reproductions under glass. In D.L. Steinberg, D. Epstein & R.

Johnson (Eds.), *Border patrols: Policing the boundaries of heterosexuality* (pp. 66-97). London: Cassell.

Stoler, A.L. (1995). *Race and the education of desire.* Durham: Duke University Press.

Stoler, A.L. (2001). Tense and tender ties: The politics of comparison in North American history and (post)colonial studies. *Journal of American History, 88,* 125-141.

Terry, J. (1999). *An American obsession: Science, medicine and homosexuality in modern society.* Chicago: University of Chicago Press.

Throckmorton, W. (2003). Dealing the race card in the gay marriage debate. Retrieved June 9, 2006, from http://gcc.savvior.com/

Walker, M.A. (1992). Feminism, ethics, and the question of theory. *Hypatia, 7,* 23-38.

Weisberg, D.K. (1993). *Feminist legal theory: Foundations.* Philadelphia: Temple University Press.

Weston, K. (1991). *Families we choose: Lesbians, gays, kinship.* New York: Columbia University Press.

Wiegman, R. (1999). Whiteness studies and the paradox of particularity. *Boundary 2, 26,* 115-150.

Wilkinson, S., & Kitzinger, C. (2006). In support of equal marriage: Why civil partnership is not enough. *Psychology of Women Section Review, 8,* 54-57.

Wright, S. (2001). *International human rights, decolonisation and globalisation: Becoming human.* New York: Routledge.

gender 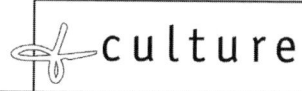**culture**

sexuality

William J. Spurlin
General Editor

This new series is a forum for the investigation and analysis of the contested terrain between culture, gender, and sexuality. Titles in the series can include, but are not limited to, (re)theorizations of gender in relation to, or its constitution through, sexuality, race, class, or culture, studies of sexuality and sexual identity that produce new understandings of gender, or new inquiries into culture, broadly defined, that raise compelling implications for the ways in which we think about gender and sexuality in the contemporary social world. Of particular interest are manuscripts that cirtique and/or broaden traditional constructions of gender and take into account sexuality, race, class, or the pressures of other constitutive categories, analyze nonwestern literary and cultural representations of gender and their relationship to sexuality, especially in postcolonial contexts, and theorize transgender from feminist, queer, postcolonial, or cultural studies frameworks.

For additional information about this series or for the submission of manuscripts, please contact:
        Peter Lang Publishing, Inc.
        29 Broadway, 18th floor
        New York, New York 10006

To order other books in this series, please contact our Customer Service Department:
        (800) 770-LANG (within the U.S.)
        (212) 647-7706 (outside the U.S.)
        (212) 647-7707 FAX

Or browse online by series:
        www.peterlang.com